Shaping Tomorrow Starting Today

The Church's Strategy For The Future

Edited by
Geoffrey Grogan

Christian Focus Publications

In the author descriptions,
the phrase 'the College' refers to the
Glasgow Bible College,
formerly the Bible Training Institute.

Scripture references are from the New International
Version, published by Hodder & Stoughton, unless
otherwise indicated.

© 1992 Glasgow Bible College

ISBN 1 85792 007 4

Published by
Christian Focus Publications Ltd
Geanies House, Fearn, Ross-shire,
IV20 1TW, Scotland, Great Britain.

Printed and bound in Great Britain by
Cox & Wyman Ltd, Reading, Berkshire

Cover design
by
Creative Link,
Edinburgh

CONTENTS

Glasgow Bible College

Founded in 1892 as the Bible Training Institute, the Glasgow Bible College is an independent institution.

It exists to serve all churches and missionary agencies, and has given full-time training to over 5,000 men and women from all over the world.

Recently, GBC secured official validation to award an Honours degree in theology, as well as Diploma and Certificates in theology.

It is unashamedly evangelical yet maintains a high standard of academic study, and plays a key part in equipping the church for its role in changing the world.

Preface

My passion to see the world evangelised will never become a reality unless we have strong local churches.

We live in the greatest period of church growth the world has ever known, but there are many obstacles and Satan is attacking every step of the way. Also, there are still thousands of people groups where the church does not yet exist. This should not be.

The people and resources are now available in our churches more than ever in history. However, apathy and disobedience are hindering the release of both people and money.

There is a danger that we may read a book just to have more knowledge when we need to take steps of faith and obey what the Word of God teaches. A man of God once said, 'There will be no gain without pain.'

Let us not be ignorant of Satan's devices (2 Cor. 2:11). He is trying to hinder and destroy the church with many strategies. Here are a few:

1. The fiery dart of impurity
2. The fiery dart of discouragement
3. The fiery dart of extremism
4. The fiery dart of false expectations
5. The fiery dart of disunity
6. The fiery dart of legalism
7. The fiery dart of false doctrine

A biblical church will teach and train her people in both defensive and offensive spiritual warfare. In Christ we can stop the enemy attacks and go forward in world evangelism and building the Kingdom across the entire world.

I have had the privilege of knowing most of the people who have contributed to this unique book and I know they are people who walk with God and who really have something important to communicate.

George Verver

INTRODUCTION

Geoffrey W Grogan

A centenary is a dangerous time for any Christian organisation. It can become a focus for nostalgia and complacent self-congratulation. There will, of course, be special events, special celebrations, but it is all too possible that real spiritual vitality has evaporated and that there is no longer any desire to change. It is the institution that has become important, not the vision.

By the time a centenary comes, not only have its founders long since died, but the succeeding generation, which inherited the vision from them, has died too. The Christian public now accepts its existence. People know that it was around as a well-established part of the Christian scene in the days of their grandparents. They have a somewhat comfortable feeling when they hear its name.

It can all add up to a recipe for stagnation.

Yes - but suppose it changes its name! That certainly makes people give it a little more thought and perhaps they may even have a vague sense of discomfort. Why has the name been changed? Has it become something different? What is happening to 'the dear old place'?

In fact a change of name may mean very little. It may simply signify a desire for a different image, but with little or no commitment to real change.

Why change anyway? Does God change, does Christ

7

change, does the Holy Spirit change? What about the Bible? Isn't that the unchanging Word of God?

Thanks be to God that he is unchanging! Not only would our salvation through Christ be at risk were this not so, but the stability and even the very existence of the universe.

We have, however, to face the fact that the world of human life changes. True, fundamental human needs do not alter, and the gospel of Christ is God's unchanging answer to those needs. Society though is constantly changing, and much more rapidly today than at any time in the past.

Not only so, but this is happening in almost every part of the world. It is becoming increasingly difficult to find any place immune from it. Look what has happened to the Communist empire, which a few years ago seemed set in concrete! If you developed an allergy to Coca Cola adverts you might have to travel a long way to be sure of finding a community where you could be sure to be out of danger.

Even very remote communities are affected in some ways. About twenty years ago I visited a tribal area where the people had recently seen a bicycle for the first time and were somewhat scared of it - but they had seen and heard aircraft flying overhead for years and now took no notice of them!

A college which trains men and women for Christian work cannot afford to remain the same. Its commitment to Christ and to the Word of God must never be in doubt, but it is preparing people for service in a constantly changing world. It dare not risk stagnation.

Read Acts chapter 7. You will find there that Stephen is saying to his Jewish audience that they were not prepared to move with God. They had become used to the solidity and seeming eternity of the temple. It gave them a comfortable feeling. But Christ had now come, and they were not prepared to move from the temple to him. God's purpose was moving on but they would not move with it. What about the Bible Training Institute - sorry, the Glasgow Bible College? Yes, its name has changed.

The great vision of its founders was for a place of training men and women for Christian service based on the unchanging gospel. This has not changed. It is precisely the vision of its leaders today.

Its commitment to eternal truth has not wavered at all. Remember that the word 'Bible' is common to both titles. The opening of a new century in the life of the College, however, brings all sorts of new challenges. The Glasgow Bible College is concerned, by God's grace, to meet them.

The chapters that follow are all written by people who have a close connection with the College. All but three are former students. The exceptions are Derek Prime and Fergus Macdonald, both of whom have been involved in the life of the College as part-time lecturers, and Peter White, who, as the present Principal, is giving fine leadership to the work. I have had the privilege of being both a student and a staff member, although not at the same time!

The themes taken up in the book are diverse but are closely related to each other. All of them concern the church. All Christian work must be intimately related to the church and it is particularly important for a College that is not linked to any particular denomination or church grouping to remember this.

The term 'church' is, of course, employed in various ways today.

It is frequently used misleadingly to designate a building. When used, more properly, of people, it is often employed for all linked to a company that professes faith in Christ. It is also used of all who have personal faith in Christ, or of all these plus their children.

It sometimes designates all Christians everywhere considered together but also a local fellowship of God's people. It is also employed of a denomination (e.g. The Methodist Church) or the Christians in one particular country (e.g. the Nigerian Church).

We must leave the reader to decide which senses best express the uses of the word in the New Testament. In the chapters that follow, it ought to be fairly simple in each case to identify from the context the sense in which it is being used.

The chapters reflect the balance to be found in the College. What is that balance?

1. It Emphasises both Christ and the Bible

The study of Scripture has a place of central importance in the work of the College. Soon after his appointment, a previous Principal, Andrew MacBeath, was shown a copy of the prospectus. He told the Board he wished to change one sentence. What was that?

The sentence declared that 'students should accept the Bible as the supreme authority in all matters of faith and practice'.

Silence!

'Yes,' he said, 'it should read, "students should accept and use the Bible as the supreme authority in all matters of faith and practice".'

Relief!

The addition was important. The College places high value on the Bible, but it expects its students to show their own respect for it by very hard work, and in their life-style.

It is important though to remember the words of Christ:

You diligently study the Scriptures because you think that by them you possess eternal life. These are the Scriptures that testify about me, yet you refuse to come to me to have life (John 5:39,40).

The purpose of Scripture is to lead us to Christ and to make us Christ-centred people. This has to be borne constantly in mind. When we study the Bible it is supremely Christ we seek. This is why the outlook of the College has been described as 'conservative evangelical'. 'Conservative' describes our attitude to the Bible and 'evangelical' the centrality of Christ and his gospel in our interpretation of it.

Does this mean then that the Glasgow Bible College is obscurantist in outlook? By no means! We face the main questions that have been raised about the Bible and find that our confidence in it as God's Word is fully justified.

Does it mean that the Bible is arbitrarily interpreted to force its every part into a kind of Christological strait-jacket? Certainly not! Scripture in fact testifies to Christ in a very wide variety of ways, and we place a lot of stress on the importance of good, sane Biblical interpretation.

2. It Seeks to Promote both Doctrine and Devotion

The study of Christian doctrine is very important and it is sad to hear it decried so often, sometimes from the pulpit by people who ought to know better.

If the gospel is not true, there is no good reason for bothering with it, but if it is, we are committed to doctrine. The gospel proclaims truth about God and human beings, about Christ and the Holy Spirit, about the cross and the resurrection, about repentance and faith, about the church and the kingdom of God.

It is vital for Christians to study Christian truth and to dedicate their minds to grappling with the profound doctrines that are taught in Scripture and that have been the precious heritage of the Christian church.

Yet doctrine is not enough. There needs to be warmth in the heart as well as light in the mind. The Christ we serve is not only the focus of great thought but also the glorious Saviour we worship and to whom and through whom we pray. A church of individual Christians that is all doctrine and no devotion is likely to be harsh, making the most winsome message the world has ever known seem cold and repulsive.

This means that the worship service and the prayer meeting have a place of importance in the life of a College alongside the theology classroom.

3. It Serves the Work of God both at Home and Overseas

There can be no room for elitism in a Bible college.

There have been times when the Christian church has valued the pastoral ministry more highly than missionary service. There are also Christians who treat the calling to overseas work as superior to the home ministry. 'The eye cannot say to the hand, ''I don't need you!'' And the head cannot say to the feet, ''I don't need you!'' ' (1 Corinthians 12:21).

The whole world is in great need. The church of Christ is God's instrument for meeting that need.

Many must go overseas. There a multitude of specialised ministries in a wide range of countries awaits men and women equipped spiritually, mentally and practically to fulfil them. These folk need to have churches behind them that are strong bases for support and that are actively engaged in mission in their own areas. These too need trained workers.

What is true is that every Christian needs to be in God's own place for him or her. We all need to be ready to serve him anywhere. Christ's commitment to us at Calvary was total. Dare we make conditions before we are prepared to serve him?

4. It Seeks to Shape Tomorrow, Starting Today

Christian service is never simply tomorrow, it is always also today. Real preparation for service should not withdraw Christian people from the world that is the place of need and God's sphere for all Christian service.

Some years ago, a brand new student stood with me at the door of the College. Looking at the people going past, he said, 'Tell me, is there still a real world out there?'

No doubt he was apprehensive that he might have joined an evangelical ghetto. I hope actual experience of the College convinced him that this was not the case.

The College is better able than ever to prepare men and women of all ages and with much variation in gift and educational background.

For many years, of course, it has done work at different academic levels, up to Honours Degree standard. The difference now is that, because of the recent official validation, it is able to offer courses leading to awards from Certificates to Honours Degrees, none of which have been created by others but all planned by the College itself. The purpose throughout has been to prepare men and women to meet the real needs of today and tomorrow, for the glory of God.

Chapter 1

The Church Of Christ Serves A Risen Lord
(The Church and Christ)

Charles Price

Charles Price is an itinerant Evangelist and Bible Teacher. He farmed in Zimbabwe for two years before returning home to England to attend Capernwray Bible School. This was followed by three years at the College, after which he became Field Representative of the Capernwray Missionary Fellowship. For eighteen years, from his base at Capernwray Hall, he has had an ever-widening international ministry. He also teaches at the Capernwray Bible School. He has spoken at the Keswick Convention and Spring Harvest. He contributes a monthly column to *Evangelism Today* and has written *Christ for Real* and *Alive in Christ*, both for Marshall Pickering, the second in association with the Keswick Convention.

Chapter 1

The Church Of Christ Serves A Risen Lord
(The Church and Christ)

Charles Price

The story is told of a multistorey building that developed a hairline crack on the wall of its forty-second floor some seven years after its construction had been completed. The managing director of the company that owned the building immediately sent for the architect who had designed it. When the architect arrived, the managing director took the lift to the forty-second floor to meet him. On his arrival, the architect was nowhere to be seen. After waiting around, the managing director returned to his office asking to be notified as soon as the architect was found. Eventually he got a message that the architect was in the sixth basement.

He took the lift to meet him and confronted him with, 'What are you doing in the sixth basement? We have a crack on the forty-second floor that we called you to investigate.' The architect replied, 'You may have a crack on the forty-second floor, but you do not have a problem on the forty-second floor; you have a problem in the basement.'

What had happened was that a security guard who worked in the building wanted to build a garage at his home but lacked both the materials and the money to purchase them. Every night before going home he took the lift down to the empty sixth basement, chiselled a brick out of the wall, put it in his bag and took it home to add to the growing pile in his garden. After several years a crack appeared in the forty-second floor!

That there are cracks on the forty-second floor of society need hardly be debated. Families are falling apart, society is fragmenting, drug abuse is increasing, diseases like AIDS are having devastating effects in some parts of the world, financial confidence is undermined and so we could go on. Solutions to individual crises are offered and are welcome, but they could be attempts to do little more than replaster the forty-second floor. There will never be lasting solutions to some of our most pressing problems until we examine the foundations upon which society is being built.

The same may be said of the church of Jesus Christ. Individual Christians are facing the same pressures as the world - and crumbling under them. Churches are often doctrinally uncertain and spiritually insecure with fragmented relationships. Talk of evangelism is a threat to individual Christians and an embarrassment to the church at large. Christian leaders are seen to collapse morally and to suffer 'burnout'. A generalisation? Yes, of course, but with enough truth seriously to concern those who take seriously the church of Christ.

Many individual solutions to individual problems might be proposed, and my observation is that many of our most popular ministries and emphases of our times are working on the forty-second floor. I suggest, however, that our major problem lies in the basement - the foundations need attention.

Paul wrote about this to the Corinthians when he told them that 'Each one should be careful how he builds ... for no one can lay any foundation other than the one already laid, which is Jesus Christ' (1 Cor. 3:10-11). Any building is as strong and as secure as its foundation and, if we wish to chip pieces out of the sufficiency of Christ, if we even minutely move the foundation on to something other than Christ, we are going to be in trouble.

I want to examine with you the relationship of the Lord
Jesus Christ to the church that is designed to make the church
the secure, vibrant and effective force it is intended to be.

The Christian Life is Christ

One of the remarkable features of the ministry of Jesus is its
self-centredness! He talked constantly about himself, whilst
paradoxically being characterised by remarkable humility! In
normal circumstances self-preoccupation is a weakness that
undermines any cause being propagated and leads others to
dismiss quickly the person concerned. But not so with Jesus.
To every need of man he offered not a programme nor a
method of improvement, but himself. To the lost he said, 'I
am the way;' to the confused, 'I am the truth;' to the hungry,
'I am the bread of life;' to those in darkness, 'I am the light
of the world;' to those on the outside, 'I am the door;' to those
needing guidance, 'I am the good shepherd;' and to the dead,
'I am the life;' To the tired and weary his invitation is, 'Come
to me' and when calling his disciples he said, 'Follow me'. It
was not an invitation to follow his programme or to adopt his
lifestyle but to follow Christ himself.

He once asked his disciples, 'Who do people say the Son
of Man is?' and then, 'Who do you say I am?' To avoid an
apparently egotistical preoccupation he might better have
asked, 'What do people think of what I say? Do they like my
teaching? Do they understand my parables?' but he didn't, for
that was not his prime concern. His concern was only their
attitude to himself.

No other religious leader has ever dared be so presumptu-
ous about himself. At best they have been able to say to the
lost, 'I will show you the way;' to the confused, 'I will teach
you the truth;' to the hungry, 'I will feed you the bread;' to
those in darkness, 'I will switch on the light;' to those outside,

'I will open the door;' to those needing guidance, 'I will give you shepherds;' and to the dead, 'I will show you where to find life'. The best they ever claim is to be the signpost - but never the way. The obvious advantage of that is that when the founder or leader dies the work can be perpetuated by others, for he himself is dispensable. The disadvantage of Jesus Christ is that if you take him away, there is nothing left! Jesus Christ claims in effect that he is himself the content of the Christian message and the substance of the Christian life.

This was the understanding of the early apostles. The apostle John wrote: 'God has given us eternal life, and this life is in his Son. He who has the Son has life; he who does not have the Son of God does not have life' (1 John 5:11-12). The 'life' cannot be separated from the Son for the life on offer is the life of the Son. It is not just that the Son is the giver of the life, he is the life!

The implications of this are far-reaching and serious for the church of Jesus Christ. We are in great danger of having once been reconciled to God by the death of Christ, and then relegating him in practice to little more than being our 'guru', at whose feet we sit and whose teaching we try to implement. We may see him primarily as our example and, therefore, the Christian life as emulation of the lifestyle of Christ. We may even relegate him to being little more than the patron of our Christianity, the one in whose name we try to live and whose flag we try to fly!

All of this is wholly inadequate and, although such approaches may contain the ingredients of religion they deny the very substance of Christianity. The truth is that Christ himself is our life, and Christianity is the living of his life in our bodies.

A significant but often overlooked change took place in the disciples the moment the church was born on the Day of

Pentecost. Prior to that they had been 'followers of Jesus'.
That was the invitation Jesus had given to them and for three
years they had faithfully tried to follow in his steps. Significantly the invitation to 'follow Jesus' was never issued after
Pentecost. That was a pre-Pentecost relationship and all it did
for the disciples, despite their genuine sincerity and integrity,
was to highlight their weaknesses!

The record only allows us to make proper comparison in
one person - Peter - before and after Pentecost. Out of all
twelve disciples, Peter is the only one who acts and speaks in
the Book of Acts. John accompanies Peter in some of his
activities and James, the brother of John, is mentioned in some
sentence when Herod put him to death (Acts 12:2). We at least
conclude that James must have been doing something worth-
while to warrant that, but we are given no details! Judas has
committed suicide and been replaced by Matthias, but of the
twelve listed in Acts chapter 1, none but Peter, John and James
get any mention later.

Few disciples were more openly enthusiastic for Jesus than
Peter. He was an impulsive talker. The Bible states of Peter,
more than all of the other disciples put together, things like
this, 'Then spoke Peter ... ' 'Up spoke Peter ... ' (the AV says,
'Peter lifted up his voice and said' ... meaning he said it
loudly!). There are times when it says, 'Then answered
Peter,' when Peter hadn't been asked anything. The only
problem was that it was invariably hot air!

Once he did state accurately who Jesus was when asked the
question, 'Who do you say that I am?' but later in the same
conversation Jesus had to say to him, 'Get behind me, Satan'
(Matt. 16:23). Six days later on the Mount of Transfiguration
he proposed building three monuments, one for Moses, one
for Elijah and one for Jesus! God intervened whilst Peter was
still talking and said, 'This is my Son whom I love ... listen to

him!' (Matt. 17:5). In other words he so much as said, 'Peter, shut up! You are talking nonsense.'

The night before Jesus was crucified he told his disciples they would all fall away on his account. Peter replied, 'Even if all fall away on account of you, I never will.' Jesus told him he would deny him three times before the cock would crow to welcome the new morning, to which he replied, 'Even if I have to die with you, I will never disown you' (Matt. 26:33-35). He was saying in effect, 'If they have to put four crosses on that hill with me on the fourth, I will be there.' Before the morning broke and the cock crowed, Peter had denied Jesus three times, and he broke down and wept. He wept at his impotence and inability to be what he wanted to be and to do what he wanted to do.

Seven weeks later the story is different. On the Day of Pentecost it was Peter who stood to explain to the crowd what was going on. I would not have been surprised if one of the other disciples had grabbed Peter by his coat and said, 'Sit down! You have said the wrong things enough times for us not to trust you with this opportunity!' But they didn't. It was a different Peter who stood at nine o'clock on the morning of the Day of Pentecost. He preached with accuracy and power, and when he finished, three thousand people believed and were added to their number. What had happened?

Had Peter learned some new techniques or some new homiletic skills? Was he now a little more disciplined than before? The truth of the matter is simple: Jesus had ceased that morning to be Peter's leader, he had instead become Peter's life! It wasn't that the church had got itself organised that day, it had become an organism that day. It was now the body of Christ indwelt by the Spirit of Christ. Organisms need organising, of course, but organisation is never the source of power. It is at best the channel through which the power that has its origin only in God is released.

After the healing of the man at the Temple Gate, Peter would say to the crowds that gathered, 'Why do you stare at us as if by our own power or godliness we had made this man walk? ... The God of our fathers has glorified his servant Jesus ... ' (Acts 3:12-13). Peter took no credit for the outcome of his ministry for he knew now he was not responsible for the transformation that came to other people. It was God at work through him.

James and John were the other two mentioned after Pentecost. They were brothers, and not very impressive! In the gospel narratives they come across as hard and arrogant. Once they asked Jesus if they should call down fire from heaven to destroy a Samaritan village that did not welcome them (Luke 9:54). They rebuked a man for driving out demons because he was not one of them (Mark 9:38). They asked Jesus to give them the two prominent places, one on his left, the other on his right, when he entered glory. When he rebuked them for not even knowing what they were asking for, they called on their mother to make the same request on their behalf! (Mark 10:35-39 and Matt. 20:20). Jesus once gave them a nickname, 'Boanerges' which meant, 'Sons of Thunder' (Mark 3:17).

Two hot-tempered, proud, arrogant young men, but the amazing thing is that John is known widely as the 'Apostle of Love' who gave us the marvellous Gospel of John and his three epistles. On the Day of Pentecost James and John ceased to be just followers of Jesus. They became incorporated into his body. He was now their life, their strength, their wisdom, their righteousness and their lives were transformed.

The Church is the Body of Christ

At Pentecost something happened to these men. They had only been followers of Jesus during the years of his ministry. During that time he had forewarned them, 'It is good for you that I go away.' I am sure they did not think it a very good idea! It would have been great to have Jesus with them the whole time, but had he remained, he would only ever be in one place at one time. He could be in Jerusalem but not simultaneously in Nazareth. He could be in Caesarea but not in Jericho. Now he told them, 'It is for your good that I am going away. Unless I go away the Counsellor will not come to you; but if I go, I will send him to you' (John 16:7).

On the Day of Pentecost he sent the Holy Spirit, and instead of merely being in the presence of the physical Christ they were baptised into Christ himself. Two things had happened at Pentecost, two things that were complementary yet distinct in their implications: the Holy Spirit had put Christ into the disciples, and the Holy Spirit had put the disciples into Christ. We are more familiar with the idea of Christ being placed into us, yet interestingly the Apostle Paul speaks more of our being 'in Christ' than of Christ being in us.

Paul tells the church in Corinth, 'You are the body of Christ' (1 Cor. 12:27). He is saying more than that the church is like a body, that the body with its many interdependent members is a good picture of the church, but that the church is actually the body of Christ in the sense that it is the place that he lives in and the means by which he works.

My body is the means by which I express myself, by which I speak and by which I work. When someone promises to be with me in spirit, I never actually notice them to be around and do not ask them to do anything! To be visible or useful it is not enough to be present in spirit, they need to bring their bodies too!

For the Lord Jesus to do his work on earth, he requires a body in which his Spirit will dwell, and through which he may operate. The Father gave him that body on the Day of Pentecost.

This is the message of Luke's opening statement in Acts, 'In my former book, Theophilus, I wrote about all that Jesus began to do and to teach ... ' (Acts 1:1). The implication is that in the second volume Luke is now writing, he is giving a record of all that Jesus continued to do and to teach, but not in his one single body in which he lived for the thirty-three years of his earthly life, but now through his new body, given him on the Day of Pentecost and called the church. It consists of men, women, boys and girls who on the basis of their repentance towards God and faith in Christ have been forgiven of their sin, indwelt by the Holy Spirit and baptised by that Spirit into Christ, now to function as his body, 'In him you too are being built together to become a dwelling in which God lives by his Spirit' (Eph. 2:22).

Everything the Lord Jesus does in the world he does through his body, through the church. He doesn't send angels to the mission field, he sends people! Angels would be a lot cheaper and certainly more effective, but they are not Christ's body and it is Christ who is at work in the work. It would be much more effective if an angel knocked on your neighbour's door to bring them the gospel than if you or I knock on our neighbour's door! The neighbours know you, they hear you shout at the children, they saw you throw the cat through the window and you feel your testimony to them is undermined! If an angel knocked on the door and just flapped his wings a little to give authenticity they would probably sit up and take notice! But that is not God's strategy in the world.

God's strategy is Christ and by virtue of being in him and a part of his body, we are the agents of his strategy. In his new body, Jesus can be actively present in Jerusalem and in

Nazareth simultaneously. He can be active in the great cities of Europe whilst at the same moment working in rural Africa. 'It is good for you that I go away.'

Christ is the Foundation of the Church

Jesus told the story of two builders who built two houses (Matt. 7:24-27). They may have used the same materials, followed the same plans and constructed seemingly identical buildings. The passer-by would admire each home equally - but only as long as the sun shone. When the rain came, the streams rose and the winds beat against each house, one fell with a great crash and the other remained intact.

The difference between the houses was invisible to the passer-by, but could not be more essential. The foundations were different. One was built on rock, the other on sand. Significantly the quality of the foundation only proved itself under pressure.

There are well-constructed, biblical-looking Christian lives which survive the fine weather but crumble in the storm. The rock and the sand in Jesus' story were in the one case obedience to his word and in the other case disobedience to his word. But the principle stands and applies to Paul's statement about the church that 'No one can lay any foundation other than the one already laid, which is Jesus Christ'.

It is true that elsewhere Paul speaks of the church 'built on the foundation of the apostles and prophets,' but he adds, 'with Jesus Christ as the chief cornerstone' (Eph. 2:20). Historically 'God spoke ... through the prophets,' and in its early days the authoritative word of the church was the 'apostles' teaching' (Acts 2:42). The prophets and apostles played an indispensable role in the process, but never as a deviation from Christ, 'the chief cornerstone'.

It is the cornerstone which determines the shape of the

building. All other stones are adjusted to the cornerstone, and the stability of the building relies on it. Paul immediately follows this statement with, 'In him the whole building is joined together ...' The stability and security of the church is derived from the position of Christ and our relationship to him. Anything that does not have its source in Christ is invalid as an expression of true spiritual life; it is merely religion.

Evangelism is not introducing people to Christianity so much as introducing them to Christ. The Christian life does not begin with theological propositions but with a person. Eternal life, said Jesus, is knowing 'you, the only true God, and Jesus Christ, whom you have sent' (John 17:3). It is being able to say with Paul, 'I know *whom* I have believed' (2 Tim. 1:12) rather than, 'I know *what* I have believed.' There is all the difference in the world between those two statements. Knowing 'what' we believe may make us doctrinally accurate yet leave us spiritually barren and powerless.

Theological propositions are important as they bring us to the person of Christ. In fact Scripture itself is only important as it brings us to Christ, as Jesus made clear in a conversation with Jews who were persecuting him for violating Scripture and healing a man on the Sabbath.

> You diligently study the Scriptures because you think that by them you possess eternal life. These are the Scriptures that testify about me, yet you refuse to come to me to have life (John 5:39-40).

His accusation was that they studied the Scriptures in order to know the Scriptures - and know them they did! If they thought anyone was stepping out of line, they pounced. Jesus was their latest victim. But they had totally missed the point. They were to study the Scriptures not primarily so that they might know the Scriptures, but so that they might know Christ.

The written Word, from Genesis onwards, is the revelation

of the Living Word. Its true function is found in its revelation to us of Christ.

At the time of writing I own a Nissan car. When I purchased it I received a manual telling me everything I needed to know about the car. I have read the manual carefully and my purpose in so doing has not been to know the manual but to know the car!

Supposing I read the manual in order to know the manual. Imagine I took a few minutes every night to read a portion and memorise a few key statements, that I joined the local Nissan fellowship where every week I would go to hear an exposition of the manual, that I organised a neighbourhood Nissan manual study group, and even put it to music to produce a book called 'Nissan in Song'. I might even become fanatical enough to study Japanese to read the manual in its original language!

I will tell you what the outcome would be. After several weeks of this kind of disciplined study of the manual, the day would come when I would say, 'I am sick of the manual.' Why? Because the purpose of the manual is not found in knowing the manual but in knowing the car!

So it is with Scripture. Jesus actually criticised the Jews for studying the Bible, because their object was only to know the Bible, when its purpose was that they might know Christ. Evangelism is introducing people to Christ. Scripture's purpose is to take us to Christ.

Christ is the Head of the Church

Christ is not only the foundation which holds the church together; he is the head who directs its activities. Paul wrote, 'He is the head of the body, the church' (Col. 1:18).

Christian work and service is not rolling up our sleeves and doing what we think best for God. Jesus once stated to his

disciples: 'The harvest is plentiful but the workers are few,'
but how were the disciples to respond to this? By committing
themselves to gathering in the harvest as best they could? No!
He said, 'Ask the Lord of the harvest, therefore, to send out
workers into his harvest field' (Matt. 9:37-38). There is a
'Lord of the Harvest'.

To follow through the metaphor of harvest which Jesus
uses, there is a farmer who knows where the harvest is and
who is capable of directing workers to the right place.
Effective evangelism is more than a hit or miss exercise, it is
allowing the Lord of the Harvest to bring us in contact with
the right people at the right time.

Soon after the church was born in Jerusalem, Philip was
preaching the gospel in Samaria with many folks turning to
Christ. Then an angel came to him and told him to leave
Samaria and to 'go south to the road - the desert road - that goes
down from Jerusalem to Gaza' (Acts 8:26). He did so and met
with the Ethiopian eunuch returning home after an apparently
fruitless visit to Jerusalem. He was a Jewish proselyte and had
gone to Jerusalem to worship, but was going home disappointed, with an open Bible on his knee.

Philip joined the chariot, explained the passage of Scripture that the man was reading and led him to Christ. The
Ethiopian was the 'harvest', Philip was the 'worker', and
bringing them together was the Lord of the Harvest.

In the following chapter, the one ripe for harvest was Saul
of Tarsus. He had met with Jesus on the Damascus road but
had apparently not yet been converted, for his sins had not
been washed away and he had not received the Holy Spirit (see
Acts 22:16 and Acts 9:17). The Lord of the Harvest looked
for a 'worker' and found one in Ananias. He sent him to Saul,
and he led him to the point of his sin being cleansed and of
being indwelt by the Spirit.

In the following chapter another man was ripe for 'harvest'. His name was Cornelius, a Gentile Roman centurion. The Lord of the Harvest looked for a 'worker' and found one in Peter, who was brought up the coast from Joppa to Caesarea where he led Cornelius to Christ.

What was the strategy in each incident? Very simply that the 'workers' allowed the Lord of the Harvest to put them in the right place at the right time for the purpose of meeting the right people - the people 'ripe for harvest'.

This continues to be the strategy. Do not leave Jesus Christ out of your strategy for evangelism! By all means knock on as many doors as you can, engage in as many personal conversations as open up to you, preach to the biggest crowds available, but never close your eyes or ears to the prompting of the Lord of the Harvest. He is the strategist, and he will have been at work in the hearts of individual people in ways you will never know, until he causes you to meet them. This is part of his business and it makes evangelism exciting!

Christ is the Life of the Church

Not only is Christ the foundation and the head of the church, he is also its very life. We have said that God's gift to us is himself and it is, therefore, in his strength that we are to operate and function. It is the reason Paul wrote:

> Not many of you were wise by human standards; not many were influential; not many were of noble birth. But God chose the foolish things of the world to shame the wise; God chose the weak things of the world to shame the strong. He chose the lowly things of this world and the despised things - and the things that are not - to nullify the things that are, so that no one may boast before him. It is because of him that you are in Christ Jesus, who has become for us wisdom from God - that is our righteousness, holiness and redemption. Therefore, as it is written, 'Let him who boasts boast in the Lord' (1 Cor. 1:26-31).

Conscious weakness is a great asset in the Christian life, for it throws us back to where we belong, in utter dependence upon God. Paul gives his own testimony to the benefit of his weaknesses when he writes of his 'thorn in the flesh, a messenger of Satan to torment me,' which he asked the Lord three times to remove from him. God's answer was not to remove it but to explain, 'My power is made perfect in weakness.' Paul then writes:

> Therefore I will boast all the more gladly about my weaknesses, so that Christ's power may rest on me. That is why, for Christ's sake, I delight in weaknesses, in insults, in hardships, in persecutions, in difficulties. For when I am weak, then I am strong (2 Cor. 12:7-10).

His power does not devalue the abilities God has given us by nature and grace. God has equipped us with gifts and abilities that we must recognise, encourage and develop. However, when our reliance is on the skills which God has entrusted to us, rather than upon God, they may be exercised skilfully - but fruitlessly! Our skills are the means by which God works, and we certainly should not ignore the need for their proper development and training, but what gives authority and life to what we do is God's own presence and his own activity. 'Apart from me you can do nothing,' (John 15:5) said Jesus, and it is possible to be very busy doing nothing if Christ is left out of the process.

Christ is the Message of the Church

The author of Hebrews writes of the progress of revelation.

> In the past God spoke to our forefathers through the prophets at many times and in various ways, but in these last days he has spoken to us by his Son ... The Son is the radiance of God's glory and the exact representation of his being, sustaining all things by his powerful word (Heb. 1:1-3).

God's last word to man is 'Jesus'. Any addition to Christ is in fact a subtraction from him, for there would only be need to add where he is deficient.

Revelation reaches its climax and its finality in Christ to the extent that Jesus claimed, 'I am the truth' (John 14:6). Truth is more than something Jesus preached, it is something he embodied. The epistles are an exegesis of him. There are many facets to truth, but every facet is in some way an expression of Christ.

The prophets who preceded Christ were revealers of truth, but they never had such a function since Christ. New Testament prophecy does not involve the giving of original truth, but exhortation and explanation of that truth which is in Christ.

The measuring stick of revealed truth is Christ. Anything purporting to come from God that is inconsistent with the Person of Christ and the accomplishments of Christ may be rejected with confidence.

The simple statement, 'The Son is the radiance of God's glory and the exact representation of his being' incorporates most of what we need to know about God's purpose for mankind. Man was made in God's 'image' which, whatever else it may entail, involves exactly representing his character. The meaning of man being in God's image is that to look at man would be to see what God is like - not physically, for God is not a physical being, but in his moral character. But man sinned and we 'fall short of the glory of God,' so that we no longer see in the behaviour of mankind what God is like.

To know what God is like and, therefore, to know what man was created to be like, we should look at Jesus who 'is the radiance of God's glory and the exact representation of his being.' Christ demonstrates in his humanity what was intended to be true of all humanity; therefore, to declare the meaning of our existence is to declare the person of Christ. To bridge the gap from what we are to what he is, required the atonement, his vicarious death, which reconciles us to God and makes possible the gift of the Holy Spirit to indwell us.

In proclaiming the meaning of life, therefore, we must preach the person of Christ and the work of Christ. Jesus said, 'I am the truth,' which is declaring something much more than 'I preach the truth.' If Christ is himself truth, then every aspect of spiritual truth is in some way an exegesis of Christ.

Christ is the Goal of the Church

Christ is the goal to which all of this is heading, for the end product of appropriating his work and receiving the gift of his Spirit is that we 'are being transformed into his likeness with ever-increasing glory, which comes from the Lord, who is the Spirit' (2 Cor. 3:18).

God's original purpose in creating man in his 'image' will find its restoration in its entirety one day, when we are fully restored into his image. This does not mean we will be 'clones' of Jesus, for we will be individual people with all the variety and richness that comes from our individual person-alities, but in our moral character we will be like Christ. Once again, as was true in the Garden of Eden, all creation looking at humankind will see what God is like, in his moral perfection and beauty.

Perhaps the greatest need of the church in every generation is to know the role of Christ himself in the Christian life. He is not only the 'author' of our faith, but also the 'finisher' (Heb. 12:2). He not only began the good work in each of our hearts, but he 'will bring it to completion' (Phil. 1:6). We could not express it more clearly than the apostle Paul when he wrote, 'For from him and through him and to him are all things' (Rom. 11:36). Everything comes from him, everything is done through him and everything is done to him. With that statement encompassing everything it raises the question, 'Where do we come in?' It is a good question, and we do come into the picture, but only as we are caught up in the activity and power of the living Christ himself, saying with Paul, 'I want to know Christ and the power of his resurrection and the fellowship of sharing in his sufferings ... ' (Phil. 3:10).

Is the forty-second floor showing some cracks? By all means plaster it, paper it and paint it but, before you do, go and check the basement. Your real problem may not be on the forty-second floor at all, it may be in the basement. Get the foundation right and you can build with unshatterable confidence on the Living Christ.

Chapter 2

And He Has Given It A Written Authority
(The Church and the Bible)

Fergus Macdonald

Rev Fergus Macdonald is a minister of the Free Church of Scotland and was the Moderator of its General Assembly in 1987. He was the minister of churches in Drumchapel, Lima (Peru) and Cumbernauld. He has been General Secretary of the National Bible Society of Scotland for the past 11 years and his work takes him to many parts of the world. He is also active in the work of the United Bible Societies and he takes a leading part in the work of the Lausanne Committee for World Evangelisation. He is the author of the book *Word Evangelism*, published by Handsel Press. He was a part-time lecturer at the College for many years and is now a member of its Board of Governors.

Chapter 2

And He Has Given It A Written Authority
(The Church and the Bible)

Fergus Macdonald

6 out of 10 British adults own a Bible, but only 2 in 100 claim to read it for pleasure.
Books and Consumer Survey 1991, conducted by Book Marketing Ltd.

The average westerner may watch the movie 'The Last Temptation of Christ' and be totally unaware what is fiction and what is fact.
James Kennedy, of 'Evangelism Explosion'

To a large extent the western church possesses a Bible, but not a Scripture.
H D Beeby

Too many Christians today do not want the Bible to interfere with their Christianity.
Brother Andrew

Today's popular ignorance of the Bible is the fruit of the strong secularising forces in western society which are particularly active in sectors such as the media, education and politics. Religion has been privatised, excluded from the mainstream of society and relegated to the week-end, weeknight world of hobbies, recreation and other forms of personal preference.

Secularisation often receives its theoretical justification from science. 'Scientist finds God an unnecessary invention' was the headline in *The Scotsman* reporting a debate held during the 1992 Edinburgh International Science Festival between the geneticist Richard Dawkins and John Habgood, Archbishop of York. The article under the six-column headline began: 'In the latest round of a centuries-old fight God lost on points in Edinburgh last night.' This trite sentence sums up the popular image of God in western media today.

But science is not the only cause of secularisation. Consumerism also is aiding and abetting the modern tendency to 'practise the absence of God'. The multiplication of individual choice and the accompanying promptings of the advertisers are creating a selfish, materialistic lifestyle which assumes life does consist of the abundance of the things we possess and is acutely embarrassed by the commandment to love our neighbour as we love ourselves.

What Hope?

In a society where God is no longer considered important, what hope is there for the Bible? In the Edinburgh Festival of Science debate, Richard Dawkins relegated the Bible's ideas and phrases to a category akin to Aesop's fables or Hans Christian Anderson's fairy tales! At best the Bible is regarded as part of the world's great literary heritage or as an ancient document highlighting one of the most potent forces behind western civilisation.

In addition to secularisation there are other forces helping to produce today's biblical illiteracy. The European Leadership Consultation in Stuttgart, called by the European Lausanne Committee in March 1992, identified three. The first is what Jacques Ellul calls 'the humiliation of the word' - the modern tendency for images to supplant words. Television, video and radio are increasing the proportion of the public who never read a book (currently one fifth in the UK) by about 1.5 per cent per annum. This is particularly the case with the people between the years of 16 and 20 where 4 out of every 10 don't open books at all. For a growing proportion of people in our society books (and consequently the Bible) are alien objects.

The second additional contributor to biblical illiteracy is the fact that our generation is the first in Europe to lose the collective memory - a memory which was sustained in past generations through story-telling (often drawing heavily from the Bible) by parents and grandparents. But television has changed all that.

A third factor, at least in more intellectual circles, is the Readers' Liberation Movement which denies that there is any stable meaning in texts and, indeed, in all media of communication. Its members claim a text has no objective meaning in itself; its meaning can be constructed only by the reader (or hearer).

A Biblically Illiterate Church!

But if this is the situation in society, surely the Bible fares better in the church! Hardly! The Life Style Survey undertaken in 1984 by the Church of Scotland Department of Social Responsibility revealed that the proportion of regular Bible readers in the churches (1 in 10) was no higher than in society generally! Why is this?

There are at least three reasons why the British church today is biblically illiterate. Firstly, rationalistic biblical criticism has robbed many Christians of their confidence in the Bible by presenting it as a complicated book beset by many inherent contradictions. Only the experts can unlock it! This repeated emphasis on the complexity of the Bible has, unwittingly, discouraged ordinary believers from reading it for themselves.

Secondly, the churches' failure to provide a popular hermeneutic (guidelines for interpreting the Bible) has led to a lot of grass-roots confusion as to what the Bible teaches. Biblical texts are quoted in support of so many differing viewpoints that it appears the Bible can be made to support all and every position! So many become sceptical about whether the Bible has anything distinctive and meaningful to say today.

Thirdly, the commendable desire to press technology into the service of communicating the gospel and the understandable tendency to focus on personal experience in seeking to authenticate the Good News is, by over-emphasis, marginalising the role of the Bible in the life and witness of many churches. Even in evangelical churches, which continue formally to affirm the supreme authority of the Scriptures, it seems to be increasingly possible to worship without the Bible being heard and to evangelise without sharing the biblical story.

This slippage of the Bible from centre stage in the evangelical world was evident even at the Lausanne II Congress, held in Manila in July 1989. Although the Scriptures were brilliantly expounded by John Stott and David Penman (who sadly died a few weeks later), they were seldom read or heard in their own right. And despite the Lausanne Covenant's high commitment to Scripture, the workshop track on using the Scriptures in world evangelization was one of the most poorly attended of all the 40 plus tracks of the Congress. On the last day of the Congress Roy Pointer shared his concern with others that the great majority could leave Lausanne II with the impression that the world can be evangelized without the Scriptures!

The Bible - A Museum Piece?
Does this prevalence of biblical illiteracy in church and society mark the beginning of the end of the Bible as a force

in the modern world? Will the Bible become an anachronism in the 21st Century?

In spite of the evidence marshalled above, I do not believe the Bible's days are numbered. Indeed, I venture to suggest we may be on the verge of a biblical revival. Why do I say this? Because there is as much evidence of awakening interest in the Bible as there is of a loss of interest.

The Bible remains the world's best-seller. At least one of its books has been translated into 2000 languages (a total which grows by the year). Global demand for copies of the Scriptures has never been higher than it is today. This hunger for the Word of God is highest in areas of explosive church growth and in the post-Marxist world.

Growing churches in mainland China, Korea, sub-Saharan Africa and in much of Latin America cannot lay hands on Scriptures in sufficient quantities to meet their needs, despite strenuous efforts by Bible publishers and distributers. Bishop Peter Hatendi of Harare speaks of 'a crocodile appetite for Bibles'. Richard Worthing-Davies of the British and Foreign Bible Society reckons that the total number of Bibles published each year is sufficient to meet the needs of only one convert in every four.

Faced with this phenomenal demand, many Bible translation and distribution agencies decided at the Lausanne II Congress to form a Forum in an attempt to multiply their effectiveness and reduce duplication. Participants include member societies of the United Bible Societies (which in the British Isles are the Bible Society in Northern Ireland, British and Foreign Bible Society, the National Bible Society of Ireland and the National Bible Society of Scotland), Wycliffe Bible Translators, International Bible Society (sponsors of the NIV), Open Doors, Pocket Testament League, Scripture Union and Scripture Gift Mission.

The recovery of civil rights by churches in the post-Marxist countries has created such a demand for Scriptures that a black market has developed! In the wake of the failure of the great Communist experiment millions are turning to the Bible in their search for values and purpose. 'It is as if people are empty; they have lost whatever idols they had. They seem to have lost their way spiritually and are now looking for the meaning of life... They want to know more about the faith of their fathers, hidden by more than 70 years of atheistic Communism; now they know they have the opportunity and are eager to seize it' (Valtra Mitskevich, Church Superintendent of the Union Council of Evangelical Christians-Baptists in the CIS). Even non-Christians like Raisa Gorbachev have stressed the value of the Bible: 'The Bible has an important contribution to make towards peace in our world, and to the moral strengthening of our people... It is important to make the Bible available now,' she said in Norway early in 1991.

But what about the western world? Even the secularised west is not without signs of a new interest in the Bible and also of new opportunities to communicate its timeless message. In the UK there is a growing demand for Study Bibles and the number of small group Bible studies is increasing. Finland and Norway are experiencing a revival of Bible story-telling on radio and in primary schools. The remarkable popularity of 'The Gospels' (a dramatised Bible reading) on BBC1 during Holy Week 1992, attracting 12 million viewers, suggests more than a passing interest in the biblical story when it is presented in the medium through which most people receive news. Norway and Finland report that, after years of decline, personal Bible reading has begun to increase.

Occasionally the power of the Bible is highlighted in our media as, for example, by Beirut hostages Terry Waite and Terry Anderson. Both acknowledged the role of the Scriptures in sustaining them throughout their long ordeal. In an interview with *Time* (18 May 1992) Terry Anderson, in answer to the question: 'What did they allow you to read in captivity?' said: 'At various times we did have a lot of books. The book I got first was the Bible, and I kept that almost throughout my captivity, though not the same copy. I read that over and over and over and over and over again and thought about it. That book was by far the most important to me and remains the most important to me.'

On a wider front, the rationalistic scientific world-view which presents the universe as a closed mechanism and which has done so much to encourage secularisation, is giving way to a more 'spiritual' view of reality. And in Western Europe, as the nations of the single market move towards closer political and social union, people are beginning to search for new values which will make the new Europe a common home as well as a common market. In this new climate of change and uncertainty people will look back as well as forward and hopefully will become conscious of the enormous extent to which Christianity and the Bible have contributed towards the development of our traditional national cultures and institutions. The building of a new Europe is presenting the churches with a unique opportunity to present the Bible as the compass for the future.

So while the Bible may be the West's least read best-seller, nevertheless, it is a best-seller; it is still highly regarded by a majority of the population; new political and philosophical trends are presenting windows of opportunity to the churches to demonstrate its relevance to the 21st Century.

What Authority?
A dynamic form of pluralism is desirable, indeed essential in a free society. But as Lesslie Newbigin has pointed out our

western pluralism has become anarchic, failing to recognise any form of absolute authority.

In this sea of moral relativism how is the church to affirm the Bible as its 'supreme standard' and as the divine norm for all peoples? For the church to do this will mean swimming against the tide. It will invite the accusation of intolerance - which the modern world regards as the cardinal sin.

If we in the church fail to affirm and to proclaim the Bible we will betray our Lord. For the church's high view of Holy Scripture is derived, not merely from creeds, confessions or councils, but from Jesus. It is he who taught that 'the Scripture cannot be broken' (i.e. annulled) (John 10:35) and affirmed that the Scripture must be fulfilled (Luke 22:37, etc). Our Lord clearly believed that the Old Testament Scriptures were infallible, i.e. they will fulfil their God-given purpose (cf Isaiah 55:11) and will not fail us. He affirmed that they were inspired by the Holy Spirit (Mark 12:35-37) and are the source of true knowledge about salvation (Matthew 22:29). His teaching was biblically based; again and again he referred his hearers to the Scriptures. He saw his teaching as fulfilling these Scriptures. See, for example, the 'Six Antitheses' of Matthew 5:17-48 where Jesus demonstrates how his teaching fulfils the Old Testament law by deepening, widening and positivising it, in sharp contrast to the shallow, narrow and negative oral tradition of the Scribes.

Jesus further taught that the Scriptures witness to him (John 5:39,40) - an affirmation which prompted John Calvin to speak of the Scriptures as 'the sceptre of Christ'. In fact, Jesus makes clear that the Scriptures are not an end in themselves; they point to him. All of us who hold to a high view of Scripture do well to remind ourselves of this lest we fall into the mistake of the Pharisees in thinking that eternal life is to be found in the Scriptures rather than in the Christ!

See John 5:39-40. In practice there ought to be no distinction between the authority of the Scriptures and the authority of Christ; it is through the Scriptures that he makes his will known to us, and it is in obedience to the Scriptures that we affirm him as our Lord.

How, then, are we to affirm the authority of Holy Scripture today? Surely this is to be done in the context of affirming Christ, and we are to affirm Christ in the context of affirming the Scriptures. An invitation to read the Scriptures is an invitation to encounter Christ in the biblical narrative. The challenge to live for Christ today is the challenge to transpose the message of the Bible into today's world.

What Purpose?

At the root of many of the problems of biblical interpretation lies a failure to relate the questions we ask of the Bible to its own self-confessed purpose. Often we ask the Bible to fulfil tasks which are outside its own 'job description' in 2 Timothy 3:15ff:

> You have known the Holy Scriptures which are able to give you the wisdom which leads to salvation through faith in Christ Jesus. All Scripture is inspired by God and is useful for teaching the truth, for rebuking error, correcting faults and giving instruction for right living, so that the person who serves God may be fully qualified and equipped to do every kind of good deed.

In other words, the Bible is a handbook of salvation and holy living.

While the Bible's focus is Jesus Christ, its basic literary format is narrative - a story which extends from creation through the fall and redemption to the consummation. It begins and ends with universal scenarios. In between it concentrates in the Old Testament on God's dealings with a single nation and in the New on Jesus Christ and his church. It presents a 'prophetic' history of Israel and the New Testament church, highlighting the principal redemptive events and drawing lessons from a series of 'case studies' involving individuals and communities.

It is this focus on events and case studies which makes the Bible a workbook for the people of God as well as a source book for the church's theologians. It is, indeed, 'the book of the unlearned' (Calvin). The model of discipleship given us by Jesus comes from the craft shop rather than from the schoolroom, for it stresses the learning of skills alongside the acquiring of knowledge. Biblical theology is applied theology.

So the Bible is very different from a book on systematic theology. Yet as Gordon Fee and Douglas Stuart remind us we sometimes forget this and treat it as if it were a collection of the 'Sayings of Chairman God'. It's much more a book about people and events than about ideas. Certainly there are ideas, but they arise out of the events; the events were not illustrative after-thoughts.

The Bible is not a text book of theology. Nor is it an encyclopaedia which holds answers to all our questions. For example, there are certain kinds of scientific questions, such as 'How old is the earth?' which it is not appropriate to put to the Bible. It is true that the Old Testament contains a number of genealogies which prompted Archbishop Ussher in the 17th century to estimate that the earth was created in 4004 BC. But scholars who have studied these genealogies in the light of ancient near eastern literature and culture, tell us that genealogies of the time focused on the most important members of the family tree, (omitting the rest) and that the recorded numbers of years people lived may have been symbolic rather than literal. There are genealogies in the Bible, not to give us an exact chronology, but to demonstrate God's faithfulness over many generations.

One of the controversies of the Reformation was whether

our galaxy is geocentric or heliocentric. The traditional view
that the earth is at the centre of our universe was defended by
many on the grounds of Genesis 1-4. Calvin, however,
warned that it is inappropriate to expect the Bible to provide
detailed answers to scientific questions. In his commentary
on Genesis he says:

> There is a certain principle that nothing is here treated of but
> the visible form of the world. He who would learn as-
> tronomy, and other recondite arts, let him go elsewhere.

Some pages further on he distinguishes between Genesis and
astronomy:

> Here lies the difference; Moses wrote in a popular style
> things which, without instruction, all ordinary persons,
> endued with common sense, are able to understand; but
> astronomers investigate with great labour whatever the
> sagacity of the human mind can comprehend.

Another misuse of the Bible is to ask it to make all our
decisions for us, as if it were a kind of spiritual horoscope.
This happens when we use Scripture texts mechanically. Let
me illustrate. Some years ago a young Christian felt God was
calling him to go to Bible School, but wasn't sure which one.
So he asked the Lord to direct him. One day he read in the Old
Testament about the cedars of Lebanon, and he took this to be
an indication that he was to go to Lebanon Bible College in
Berwick. This is hardly a satisfactory method of interpreting
the Bible if only because it rules out the many Bible Colleges
which lack a biblical name!
     One final example of misuse of Scripture is when we treat
it as if it were a charm. During the First and Second World
Wars some soldiers carried small pocket Bibles or Testaments

in their tunic pocket in the hope that somehow this would protect them in danger. More recently an Indonesian mother left her toddler alone in the house, asking her Bible to look after it. Sadly the child fell into the fire and got severely burned. When she returned, the mother held up her Bible, looked at it and said: 'You've failed'! It is still a custom in parts of West Africa for Christians, when building a new house, to bury a copy of the Bible in each of the four corners of the foundation in an attempt to ward off evil spirits.

But the Bible is not a charm; it is not a horoscope; it is not an encyclopaedia; it is not a theological textbook. Rather it is a handbook and workbook to guide us as to how to become Christians and live as disciples. There is no area of living over which it does not exert its authority, but it does this as a handbook and a workbook and not as a specialist textbook. It's like the handbook we receive with a new car, or a new television set. It contains our Maker's instructions as to how we are to operate. And we constantly need to consult it, for our lives don't work well because of sin. Things regularly go wrong and we need to go back to the handbook to get them right.

What Sense?

We have already observed that the Bible can be used to prove almost any point of view. We now come to consider guidelines for interpreting it. The science of interpretation is called 'hermeneutics'. Unfortunately discussion in this area is often carried out in a rather rarefied academic atmosphere, and - as we have already suggested - one of the urgent needs of the hour is for the development of a popular hermeneutic which will help the people of God find for themselves the meaning of what they read in the Bible.

The Reformation succeeded in making the Bible the book of the people precisely because the reformers worked out a popular hermeneutic which enabled ordinary people to access the Scriptures for themselves and apply them in their daily lives. The reformers' secret was that they believed the Bible is to be interpreted in its *natural* or *plain* sense. One way of ascertaining this is to ask what was the meaning intended by the biblical writer.

This is very different from a *literalistic* approach to the Bible which ignores the literary form of the passage and the culture within which it was written. For example, Christians who see the psalmist's references to his kidneys ('reins') instructing him as a basis for constructing a biblical science of psychology, are guilty of violating the poetic genre and figurative language of the psalms.

Making the natural sense of Scripture paramount has three great advantages. Firstly it takes the literary qualities of the Bible seriously. It recognises the Scriptures' literary pluralism evidenced in the presence of parable, poetry, proverbs, genealogies, letters, riddles, laws and sermons as distinct literary genre in addition to narrative. It refuses to separate the content (what is communicated) from its form or genre (how it is communicated). It attempts to approach each book, passage, text as a literary whole.

Secondly, the emphasis on the natural sense does justice to the biblical books as historical documents. The focus upon the plain sense of each biblical narrative allows the factual historical and geographical references contained in it to be evaluated on their merits rather than being immediately suspect as possible literary inventions. The plain sense assumes that things are as the text says they are and, that, if symbolism is present, it enhances rather than diminishes the text.

The complement of this is that 'hard' extra-biblical historical data often confirms the natural sense. For example, twenty-five Hittite international treaties (or covenants) dating

from the second millennium BC contain many literary similarities to the Book of Deuteronomy, suggesting that this book
belongs to the Mosaic period from which it claims to come
rather than from the considerably later period allocated to it
by many biblical scholars. Similarly, the structural similarities
between the Book of Exodus and the Ugaritic epics discovered
at Ras Shamra in modern Syria suggest that Exodus is substan-
tially a literary unity rather than a patchwork document.

The third advantage of highlighting the natural sense is that
it opens up the Scriptures to ordinary Christians. Although the
plain sense of a passage is not always immediately apparent
on a cursory reading, in most cases the broad sense of a
biblical book or of a section within it can be discerned by
careful and thoughtful study.

Concordances, word lists, expository preaching, commen-
taries and dictionaries can help enormously, enriching, en-
larging (and sometimes modifying) an initial natural appre-
ciation of a given passage, but they are not essential for a true
understanding of Holy Scripture. In contrast those who argue
that the natural or plain sense is not the true sense of Scripture,
telling us that the real meaning is hidden by symbolism of the
language or conflation of the sources, make popular users of
the Bible totally dependent on the experts and often hinder a
direct encounter with the Word of God.

What Next?

In his vivid parable of the two houses (Matthew 7:24-27)
Jesus underlines for us that hearing the Word is not enough.

So the question 'What next?' is vital. What the church does
with the Bible tells us more about its witness than what it says
about it. Truth, in the Bible, is something we *do* as well as
something we *believe*!

The practical challenge facing the Church in relation to the

Bible is two-fold: to develop biblical literacy within its fellowship and to facilitate biblical witness by its members to the world.

Biblical Literacy

It is helpful to think of three levels of biblical literacy: basic, functional and highly functional.

A *basic biblical literate* is someone who is aware of the division of the Bible into two Testaments and of the New Testament into Gospels, Acts and Letters; who has read through at least one of the biblical books; and who can locate Abraham, Moses, Jesus and Paul in the biblical story.

A *functional biblical literate*, in addition, reads a passage of Scripture once or more a week, and knows the overall shape of the biblical story (Adam & Eve - Garden of Eden - Flood - Abraham - Joseph - Moses - Exodus - Desert wanderings - Conquest - Kingdom - David - Prophets - Exile - Jesus [birth, ministry, death, resurrection, ascension] - Pentecost - New Testament church - Apostles - Book of Revelation); and who knows where to locate any book in the Bible without consulting the contents page.

A *highly functional biblical literate*, in addition, reads the Bible daily and systematically, uses a popular hermeneutic and is aware of the principal themes of the Bible (Creation - Sin - Salvation - Discipleship - Judgment - Eternal life).

No doubt these definitions can be improved upon, but they give us objective standards against which we can measure our own biblical literacy and that of others.

How can a church set about becoming biblically literate? During his thirteen years as pastor of Nairobi Baptist Church, Tom Houston consciously set himself the goal of making his congregation biblically literate. Here is his own account of how he did it:

We worked from the basis that in 2 Timothy 3:14-17 there were four functions and four disciplines with regard to Scripture.

The four functions are: (a) To lead us to Christ and to salvation; (b) To teach us truth and correct error, (which I take to mean modifying the worldview people start out with); (c) To show us right and wrong behaviour; and (d) To make us good at our work.

The four disciplines are: (a) Becoming acquainted with the Scriptures; (b) Learning them, (which I understand to mean the ability to play these back); (c) Becoming fully convinced of the truths of Scripture, (which I take to mean testing them in the experiences of life); (d) Continuing in these disciplines for a whole lifetime.

I had a major drive every year to get people into *reading the Scriptures through*. On Bible Sunday, the second Sunday in Advent, we promoted Scripture Union notes for all ages. Every organisation in the church was involved in this drive to get more people than ever before lined up for Bible reading on January 1 of the following year. We eventually had about 250 people taking Scripture Union notes.

In the *Sunday School* we used the lesson materials that were most biblically related and encouraged the children in Scripture memory.

In all the *Sunday Services* I expounded the Scriptures consecutively in extended series, and over the twelve years covered in detail one third of the text of the Old Testament and two thirds of the text of the New. This was done in a highly contextualised fashion, covering sooner or later every facet of life. This meant that people were getting a biblical worldview over against the worldview with which they had grown up in their various cultures, for it was a multiracial congregation. They could, therefore, locate the issues that arose from the experiences they encountered in their daily lives. It also meant that they got used to the structure of the Bible by osmosis.

I put the whole biblical text being expounded on an
overhead projector so the congregation could see on the
screen my marking and underlining the text in order to get
at its meaning.

We also had *home study groups*, as many as 19 at one
time. I kept in touch with the leaders and helped them to
prepare biblical material. Following good group dynamic
principles, they made the choice of the passage for study
with their group.

We started a *Youth Church* and involved the musical
young people in biblical communication through Scripture
in song. We challenged those who could write or act or help
with drama to dramatize Scripture every week in the service.
They were given the story to dramatize and they did the
scripts which were often very powerful and an aid to the
exposition which followed.

This foundation laid twenty years ago continues to bear fruit.
A survey of the congregation carried out in 1991 showed that
44% of the members were reading the Bible daily.

Developing biblically literate congregations is one of the
most important tasks confronting the churches in Europe and
North America at the end of the 20th Century.

A Popular Biblical Hermeneutic

Before leaving this subject it might be helpful to unpack a
little the phrase 'popular hermeneutic' which has cropped up
several times earlier in the chapter. By this we mean a simple
method of interpreting passages of Scripture and discerning
their meaning in the course of our personal reading of the
Bible.

The popular hermeneutic of the Reformers and their
immediate successors is summed up by the Westminster
Confession of Faith:

> The infallible rule of interpretation of scripture is the scripture itself; and therefore, where there is a question about the true and full sense of any scripture (which is not manifold, but one) it must be searched and known by other places that speak more clearly (I.x).

Assuming that the true sense of Scripture is its natural or plain sense is an important first step. But it doesn't solve all our problems, for sometimes it appears that some Scriptures - even in their plain sense - disagree with other Scriptures. This tension within the Scriptures is not surprising. They are not, after all, written in the style of a do-it-yourself manual. Rather they are a library of 66 books, containing a variety of literary forms, written by a wide variety of authors over many centuries.

Because all Scripture is inspired by God it has a basic unity and harmony. So if we interpret Scripture by Scripture, taking into account the literary form and historical background in each case we should come to understand what the Scriptures as a whole are teaching.

We can illustrate this from the differing emphasis in James and Paul on the relationship between faith and works. Paul insists that 'a person is put right with God only through faith, and not by doing what the Law commands' (Romans 3:28). On the other hand, James claims 'that it is by his actions that a person is put right with God, and not by his faith alone' (James 2:24). Superficially they appear to be on a collision course. But if we compare carefully the two passages we discover that faith is being used in a different sense in each. For Paul in Romans faith is the trust in God which Abraham exhibited; but for James faith is of a much more general type which even demons share (2:19). Paul uses faith in the sense of trust and James in the sense of mental acceptance. Martin Luther concluded from both passages that the Bible teaches that we are put right with God by faith alone, but not by a faith that is alone, for it produces godly works.

When we interpret Scripture by Scripture it is helpful to follow five simple rules: First, the New Testament is to interpret the Old; second, the teaching passages are to interpret the incidental; third, universal passages are to interpret passages dealing with local and cultural practices; fourth, clear passages are to interpret the unclear, and, fifth, Jesus' words in John 16:12,13 indicate that the Epistles ought to be interpreted as a continuation of his teaching in the Gospels.

In addition to helping to resolve the problem created by conflicting messages in the Bible, a popular hermeneutic will provide clues which will enable us to cross the culture gap existing between our world today and the world of the Bible, a gap which can make the Bible appear so strange to late 20th Century people. The key here is to know how to interpret the various literary forms ('genre') in the way appropriate to each genre which has its own rules for making sense. Poetry, for example, is to be interpreted differently from narrative, prophecy from parable, etc. Kevin Vanhoozer of New College, Edinburgh compares the biblical genre to different kinds of maps. Only when we know the kind of map we have do we discover where we're going. A popular hermeneutic will enable readers to identify the different 'maps' used by the biblical writers.

Finally, a popular hermeneutic will suggest some basic steps which will enable us to relate the message of the Bible to our situation. After all, the purpose of the Bible is practical: it's a handbook of salvation which ought to exercise a controlling influence on our beliefs, our behaviour and our work (2 Timothy 3:15,16). So understanding the meaning of a passage of Scripture is not enough. The Word must be applied as well as read and heard. There are three simple steps in applying Scripture to our lives. First, we are to *internalise* it. When we read a passage of Scripture we consciously need to take it to ourselves and ask God to speak to us through it. Second, we are to *contextualise* it by applying it to our context or situation. We ask God to show us how the passage applies to our situation. Third, we are to *actualise* it by obeying the Word and living it out.

Biblical Witnessing

The second challenge facing the churches is to equip their members to share the Scriptures with others. Christianity in the early church was spread as much by the Christians as by the apostles. Following Stephen's martyrdom 'the church in Jerusalem began to suffer cruel persecution. All the believers, except the apostles, were scattered throughout the provinces of Judaea and Samaria... The believers who were scattered went everywhere, preaching the message' (Acts 8:1,4).

The pattern is much the same today. In areas of the world where the church is growing this is largely happening through the witness of ordinary Christians. Of course, church services and evangelistic missions also play an important role, but research indicates that the great majority of unbelievers who come to church or to an evangelistic meeting are invited and brought by their Christian friends.

In South Korea, which has witnessed some of the most dramatic church growth anywhere this century, many congregations issue their members with a packet of Scripture leaflets every month for distribution to their non-Christian acquaintances. Church members are expected to use these; it's part and parcel of their membership. Fifty million of these leaflets are distributed every year and the churches which use them are among the fastest growing in the country.

In many African countries Christians will, almost as a matter of course, share what they learn in their daily Bible reading with the people they meet in the course of the day.

And they will tell how their Bible reading helped them to overcome a problem or undertake a difficult task. They are not content (as we often are) to read the Bible for consumption; they also read it for communication - to have a word from the Lord to share with others. As in Korea, so in Africa, this biblical witness is accompanied by dramatic church growth.

What these Christians of the younger churches are doing is demonstrating the correlation between the sowing of the Word of God and the growth of the Kingdom of God which Jesus teaches in the parable of the Sower (Mark 4:1-9;13-20). It is as the Good Seed is sown that people acknowledge the Kingship of God.

In this 'Decade of Evangelism' our British churches must learn this secret of growth from the younger churches. We must equip and mobilise our people to live their lives out of the Word and to witness with that Word to others. 'Word Evangelism' is one of the priorities of the hour!

The churches' biblical witness must be addressed to society as well as to individuals within it. At the beginning of this chapter we touched on the opportunities the development of the new single market is presenting for biblical witness to Europe. Now as we draw this survey of the church and the Bible to a close I wish to describe in more detail the unique opportunities of this moment in our history.

Lesslie Newbigin quotes the verdict of the Hungarian scientist, Michael Polanyi, that the past 300 years have been the most brilliant in all human history - a brilliance which was achieved, according to Polanyi, by the combustion of a thousand years of Christian tradition in the oxygen of Greek rational thought. But the brilliance has dulled, and Newbigin claims western society is in crisis today precisely because the fuel is now exhausted; pumping in more oxygen is not producing new light!

The question Bishop Newbigin is challenging the churches to ask is: 'How do we replenish the fuel?'

Surely the place to begin is the Bible for it is the Good News of Jesus Christ which contains the fuel the West desperately needs if it is to find a role and a purpose in the world which will serve the whole of humanity and glorify God. This is why it is vital that the churches encourage all Christians to make every effort to present the Bible as containing a message for today and tomorrow.

This is a difficult task because it will involve us, not only in reading the Bible, but also through our reading and hearing it, in working out a biblical worldview and in developing a Christian mind so that our perception of life, our motivation in living and our pattern of conduct will begin to reflect the extraordinary living which Jesus illustrates in the Sermon on the Mount.

But although following the Bible as the way ahead will be difficult, surely it is possible!

Possible because we will be sharing and following the Word of God which, as the sword of the Holy Spirit, can penetrate and demolish the strongest defences of inertia and unbelief.

Possible because we will be sharing and following the Word of God, which as the seed of Christ's Kingdom, can bring new life and growth where none existed before.

Possible because we will be following and communicating Scriptures which, in the words of John Calvin, provide us with spectacles through which to interpret the world and to live in it for God's glory.

May we go into the future with this Word in our hands and in our hearts, discovering it afresh each day to be to us sword, seed and spectacles in our service for the Lord!

Chapter 3

Calling It To Worship
(The Church and Worship)

C Peter White

Rev Peter White was appointed principal of the Glasgow Bible College in 1990. He qualified first as a veterinary surgeon but after his conversion was called to the Church of Scotland ministry. He trained for both at Glasgow University, winning a number of prizes during his theology course. From 1974-90 he was minister of St David's Broomhouse, a housing scheme church in Edinburgh, and in that context trained several probationers for ministry. He has wide experience in various types of chaplaincy work and is interested in AIDS education and also in a housing project for mentally handicapped adults. His academic involvements have included the Scottish Tyndale Fellowship and Rutherford House, and he has written for Christian Focus Publications.

Chapter 3

Calling It To Worship
(The Church and Worship)

C Peter White

'English services are more serious than Scottish, aren't they Dad?' said our ten year old after holiday this year. It was the word 'serious' which struck me. We had staggered through the intricacies of the Alternative Service Book and heard sermons which by Scottish standards were brief and light-weight. What was more serious about that? Or less serious about the Church of Scotland services - evangelical with meaty sermons - she normally attends? 'Serious' seemed to mean solemn or formal, and to describe the difference between ritual and our less explicit Scottish structure.

Worship is the current buzz word in British Christianity. Every denomination and fellowship is discussing it. What makes for living, church-building worship? Which issues in worship are incidental and which fundamental? What do we think of inter-faith worship? How much movement and excitement and what musical ethos are appropriate? An evangelical Bishop recently caused a furore by publicly declaring 'twice is enough' when it comes to the repetition of choruses. If more than one or two persons are up front giving the lead is that degeneration into performance or an improvement in participation?

I have made it part of my job to attend worship in as wide a range of situations as I can find consistent with dependable commitment to my own church. I have attended charismatic, catholic and reformed, denominational and non-denominational, formal and free. I have waved, clapped, knelt, stood, danced (a little) and sat through good and bad. What has become clear is that there would be great benefit if Christian groups consistently planned and practised worship in accordance with its most important biblical and theological guidelines. The purpose of this chapter is to suggest some essential ones and to plead for their application.

1. Worship is humanity's most necessary and climactic activity

God is our maker, great and attractive and utterly perfect. We are his creatures and our chief reason for existing is to glorify and enjoy him. In considering worship we are not dealing with a supplemental or side issue in human experience. This is evident not only from the consideration of who we are and who God is, but also from the command underlined by our Lord, 'You shall worship the Lord your God, and him only shall you serve.'

Add to this that God speaks of his people as having been formed for himself to declare his praise (Is. 43:21; 1 Peter 2:9f) and speaks also of inhabiting or being enthroned upon the praises of his people (Ps. 22:3); that he has so arranged human life that one day in seven is to be set apart for him in a rest from other things; and it is clear that worship is the biggest, most important thing we ever do. Worship is the greatest activity of humankind.

2. What do we mean by worship?

The word comes from an old English word 'worth-ship': to accord God his worth or value, to make recognition of his worthiness. The meaning of the main words translated 'worship', in both Old and New Testaments, is to bow oneself down, to prostrate oneself, to 'kiss (the dust) in front of.' The cardinal test of a time of worship is, whether that is what is going on.

The primary question is not 'are we enjoying ourselves?' but 'are our hearts bowed, our lives quite at the disposal of this great King, our God to whom we are paying homage?' In the words of the Puritan writer Stephen Charnock, 'When we believe that we should be satisfied rather than God glorified, we put God below ourselves, as though he had been made for us rather than we for him.'[1] This is not to say that hearty worship is not satisfying; it is to insist that the very meaning of the word 'worship' lays an onus on us to come to worship orientated towards God rather than self: a commitment to honour him and find it sufficient to have done so.

Think of the difference such an approach would make. Would it not root out much grumbling and criticism? You didn't enjoy that hymn? - it wasn't for you, it was for God, and if you gave it to him with all your heart and strength, that's all that is needed. Your pleasures are not the measure of the hymn!

Would it not also root out the 'spectator-performance problem?' Derek Kidner has a typically pithy comment on Psalm 22:3 (God is enthroned on the praises of Israel): 'The metaphor also puts the question to the church, whether its hymnody is a throne for God or a platform for man.'[2] A service recently broadcast on television from a prominent church closed, I am told, with the music group performing a jazz piece and presumably being clapped for it. I should have thought the test for it as worship would be Kidner's and the test of its effectiveness, did it produce a sense of God, a spontaneous bowing before his majesty?

The commonest biblical words for worship mean to bow oneself down in homage, as we have seen. But the other words used for this activity are also important because they point up its significance. They mean 'service' and are used equally of doing the chores, religious gatherings and voluntary work in the community. This has two messages for us:

First, worship is service. The most important service that we render God, is the responsive love and honour we give him in worship. That is why we call worship times 'services': they really are our most important service of him.

Does not the lovely metaphor of the church as the Bride of Christ help here? No true lover wants a wife for what she can do for him, but just that she can be his, and he hers, in love. And so it is with Christ's love for us. Of course in our gratitude we want to go out in practical service for him and it is part of Christian obedience to do so. But he made us his own to present us to himself in splendour, not because of our usefulness! Let us recognise then the centrality, the dignity of worship, and give it the priority and best attention which are its due.

Secondly, service is worship. The Bible does not permit the view that practical service is less holy than, say, times of worship. To offer God our bodies in living sacrifice is both our reasonable service of him (Rom.12:1, AV and RAV) and a spiritual act of worship (NIV).

Must we widen our definition of worship, then, to include everything we do; and if so, what currency does it have?

When we are thinking of worship we must distinguish between the generic and the specific. The generic is the devotion we owe to God in the whole of life. The specific is the exercise of worship in the specialised sense - prayer, thanksgiving, reading the Word, preaching, singing God's praises, administering the sacraments. [3]

(a) Worship in the generic sense
'Whatever you do, work at it with all your heart, as working for the Lord, not for men' says Paul (Col. 3:23), and 'Whether

you eat or drink, or whatever you do, do all to the glory of God'
(1 Cor. 10:31). Here is *life* as worship: liturgical living, if you
like. The notice, 'Divine Service three times a day' has been
seen pinned over the washing-up bowl. Are our lives all they
should be? It has been said, for example, that if you put a
professing Christian behind a steering wheel he becomes a
tiger, so many of us are discourteous and illegal drivers. Well,
the principle of liturgical living calls us to consistent practical
Christianity!

Does the notion of generic worship help us evaluate an
issue already mentioned, the musical performance that was
used to conclude a time of worship? The musicians were
playing to the glory of God. Musicianship is their (generic)
worship as washing up and brain surgery are other people's.
As much, yes, but not more than: is there perhaps a certain
danger in incorporating performance in worship? People
have gathered - let them enjoy music, or snooker, or anything
else for which people assemble to be spectators of others'
expertise. But to the extent that it is in danger of being a
platform for man or of implying that one activity (musical
performance) is more 'worship' in this generic sense than
another (would they be as likely to clap potato peeling, cement
mixing or Scalextric racing?), to that extent it seems to me a
confusion of categories.

There is another crisis for us in the principle that all of life
is worship. Our consistency as Christians dynamically affects
our worship in the specific sense, and therefore our fellowship
with God. Time and again the prophets, and our Lord Jesus
especially, draw attention to this. 'My soul hates your festi-
vals, feasts and convocations,' said God to the Jewish people
on one occasion. And why? Because they were failing to seek
justice, encourage the oppressed and defend the cause of the
widow and orphan (Is. 1:11-17). Unkindness, immorality,

hardness of heart, lack of generosity - these lead to our worship being rejected, our prayers not heard, our lives limited. Let's put that positively - the generosity of our lives, the quality of our relationships, the integrity between our beliefs and behaviour, these constitute doors of opportunity for life, power and reality in the church's worship. Let us make our generic and our specific worship one seamless whole for Jesus.

(b) Worship in the specific sense
If all that we do is to be service of God and thus worship in that generic sense, there is also specific worship when we draw aside from all else to be with God and engage in the activities that characterise times of devotion. Specific worship can again be divided into public and private worship. The latter deserves a treatment of its own and is not further addressed in this chapter, concerned as we are with the church and worship.

To summarise this section: we can distinguish between the generic sense of worship which means serving God in all we do, and its specific sense, that giving of ourselves to those times when we bow ourselves before him in the activities of 'conscious, wholehearted offering to God of the honour and homage which belong exclusively to him,'[4] either in private or together as a church. These considerations challenge us concerning the consistency between our whole life and our Christian profession, and as to the living reverence and homage with which we carry out our individual and corporate worship.

3. Jesus is at the heart of all Christian worship
Jesus is God the Son, the second person in the Trinity. God - Father, Son and Holy Spirit - is the one object of our worship, and so our Lord is at the heart of our worship in that sense. But

Jesus is also truly man, the only person who has ever worshipped God perfectly. We owe God worship, we want to glorify and enjoy him, but we fall short. God graciously provides, in Christ, the perfect worship we owe him.

The two movements in worship (of which more anon) - God to us, we to God - are alike full of Jesus. God comes to us in Christ: in the incarnation, audibly in the Word read and preached, to all five senses in the bread and wine of the Lord's Supper. And even our response is full of Jesus: God does not throw us back on ourselves to make our response unaided (and so fail), but gives us 'in the Man Jesus that response which alone is acceptable to Him.'[5] It is still we who worship; and yet 'no worship has ever pleased God except that which looked to Christ.'[6] So authentic worship is absolutely full of Jesus. He is the object of worship as a Person of the Godhead, the only successful worshipper, the mediator and perfecter of the worship that we offer. The theme is glorious and worth exploring.

First, Jesus is the foundation who makes worship possible at all. We know that of ourselves we are sinners, our natures tainted by self-centredness and our deeds by guilt. But lo! Our King Jesus has lived the perfect life that can be our righteousness before God, and he died the atoning death that wipes our guilt away. In faith and at God's invitation we make the wonderful exchange, swapping our sins and sin (that we hand over to him) for his Son (whom he holds out to us). So we become God's friends, righteous in his sight. Our Lord Jesus leads us by the hand into God's very presence as we come to worship. This is the only way there: 'No-one comes to the Father but through me' (John 14:6). Jesus is thus the reconciler of man to God, the foundation without whom acceptable worship is impossible.

The issue of inter-faith worship seems solved at a stroke.

People are sharing in worship when they worship God through Jesus in the Spirit. Unless they come through Jesus they are not coming to the Father whatever else they are doing, and if they are not Christians they do not have the Spirit of Christ (Rom. 8:9) and so are not coming in the Spirit. Interfaith dialogue, gracious and faithful, is a great task; but between Christian and non-Christian worship there is a great gulf fixed: they are simply different activities.

Is it not cruel to suggest otherwise? God through Jeremiah condemns the practice of saying 'peace, peace' when there is no peace with God (Jer. 6:14; 8:11): what could be more cruel than to assure a person in danger that he is safe? Is it not kinder to inform and invite? (Acts 2:22-40). Can we imagine Elijah kneeling side by side with the prophets of Baal, or Paul writing 'let darkness and light join in inter-faith partnership in worship'?

Secondly, Jesus models and presents our worship. Is a person uncertain how to pray or whether he or she can know God personally? Let them look to Jesus - *his* example can be trusted if nobody else's can. What do they see? A man looking up into his Father's face and saying 'Abba': 'dear Father'. They see a man who was dependably at public worship (Luke 4:16). Jesus is a model for us.

Jesus also offers our worship in the true sanctuary, God's nearer presence (Heb. 8:2). Part of his work as our High Priest is to take on himself all the guilt and shortfall in what we offer, so that it is accepted by God (Ex. 28:38). By virtue of our union with Christ, we are there in the heavenly sanctuary, offering worship acceptable to God through Jesus Christ, our mediator and representative.

See how pride and shame are equally excluded. Pride - for all we do falls short and is acceptable because Christ offers it to God. Shame - for we are there in the person of Jesus, in union with him, and through him what we offer is atoned for and perfect!

4. Times of worship should have both passion and structure

Here is my burden. It is possible to attend worship expectantly, with prayer and self-preparation, yet come away dulled and disappointed. In my experience the service has lacked either life or design. I make three pleas.

First, let's have some passion! I address pastors and people alike and regret to say that there are many evangelicals, self-styled, who need the appeal quite as much as others.

Worship is the most urgent, momentous activity of our lives. Is that reflected in the urgency we bring to it? Here are some words, addressed perhaps to worship leaders in the first instance, but of general application, from the Rev. William Still:

> It is not the form of worship which is of primary importance, but the presence of the Holy Spirit in the fullness of his power: it is that which makes any service live. The most ordinary style of Presbyterian worship can be fraught with incalculable help and blessing if the Holy Spirit is permitted to release himself and is honoured in it.
>
> What the Spirit does is to infuse into the staidest form of worship such liveliness as will quicken all regenerate souls and make them sit up and take notice - and probably startle others too!
>
> And the way he will do it is by quickening the Lord's servant to such a degree that his voice becomes more lively, more interestingly modulated and his words more clearly articulated - he is on his toes - and he will incline to use the most satisfying language to cloke his thoughts, both in prayer and in the sermon. But the very way he introduces worship will arrest attention, and the praise will tend to

inspire and not depress the people, and when he comes to read the Scriptures, it will be clear that he is more than reading them: he is living them! [7]

If the above words apply primarily to pastors we, the people, owe worship a corresponding commitment. Let us pray earnestly for the minister and his preparation during the week. Let us go to bed early enough on Friday and Saturday nights to be awake on Sunday mornings. Let us come expectant, wanting to learn, willing to work at the two movements in worship (God to us, we to him). Let us not wait to see if the sermon is good or the preacher on form, but make it our business to understand what he is saying, commit it to memory and obey what God has said to us through him. Let us so give ourselves to responsive praise that we are exhausted by the end of a service.

Secondly, let's make a place for contribution and freedom somewhere in the worship life of a church. Some will think this too modest an application of 1 Cor. 14:26-40, but I have in mind that the majority of the churches in Britain are long established with well-tried orders of service. The main (perhaps only) Sunday service is not necessarily the place to introduce this element, at least not in any major way and not at first. But as I read the New Testament it is the irresistible implicate of the priesthood of all believers. If we are a priesthood it just will not do that only one person ever gives voice in prayer when the church assembles. It's a strange family that appoints just one person to talk to Father. And not just in prayer, but in other ways we should surely arrange to benefit from the contributions some have for the worship life of the church. Cyril Ashton's book *Church on the Threshold* describes how one Anglican vicar delivered these principles (albeit held radically) into the life of a traditional congregation.

Thirdly, let services have a structure. Paul Beasley-Murray comments, 'The sense of movement implicit in some of the traditional orders of service has been abandoned, and little of substance has been put in their place.'[8] I have to say that that has been my observation also. Sometimes a service has consisted almost exclusively of a number of songs each repeated several times, followed by the preaching and departure. What would the Bible say to this?

Look at worship in the Old Testament: structure is clearly built into it. The very architecture of Tabernacle and Temple speak of several reasonable stages: *preparation*, made careful by the enormous attention to detail (e.g. Ex. 25-31 and 35-40, Lev. 1-9), the removal of one's shoes because coming to holy ground, and the sanction visited upon the careless (Lev.10); *approach*, involving a sacrifice to atone for sins; *prayers*, emphasised by the visual aid of presenting incense. Throughout Old Testament times, similarly, the *word of God* to his people was more basic to their existence even than food: 'Man does not live by bread alone, but by every utterance of the mouth of the LORD' (Deut.8:3). *Psalm singing*, probably antiphonal, also featured at least in later Old Testament worship, ending with the Aaronic *blessing* (Numbers 6:22-27) and *departure*.

Worship, in other words, has sequence and contains certain essential ingredients. It is made real, of course, not by the events of themselves but by the love of God and the people's responsive love and thanks (Deut.7:6-11; 11:13; Micah 6:8).

The New Testament gives us, certainly, fewer guidelines on how to structure times of worship. Yet in instituting the Lord's Supper Jesus modelled it on the structure of the Passover service and gave it proper planning, preparation, teaching, actions and order, with closing hymn (Matt. 26:17-30). The church clearly followed him in this basic continuity

with and Christian development of the principles of worship
found in the Old Testament (Acts 2:46). It was the norm to
meet on the first day of the week, clearly the Christian's new
living out of the Sabbath principle, and spend time which
included the breaking of bread and sustained teaching (Acts
20:7-12).

The Apostles taught thoroughly about worship including
its content and significance, the need for orderliness, understanding and order and the crucial centrality of concern for the
poor and social justice between Christians which we have
already seen as integral to acceptable worship (1 Cor. 10:15-
22; 11:17-34; 14:1-40).

Even if we took the Bible alone, therefore, and ignored the
subsequent 2,000 years of history as though the life of the
church under the Spirit could teach us nothing, we should
conclude that times of worship would best be well planned
and structured; and the content would regularly include
singing, the reading and prophetic-didactic exposition of
Scripture, prayers and the breaking of bread. The New
Testament does not insist that 'breaking of bread' is weekly
- it was initiated at Passover time, after all - but the irresistible
impression is that it was so practised in New Testament times.

If in addition, as I affirm, we are wise to take seriously the
subsequent historical life of the church, the lesson is underlined. Space forbids development of this theme but it is worth
considering how the Spirit has led the church (and how the
church has dried up and needed reviving in these matters). Let
us study and apply the principles of liturgy, always emphasising
that what it is about is the inner reality: the honour of God, the
Saviourhood of Jesus, the love of our hearts.

I appeal, therefore, to those who leave the shape and order
of worship times unplanned in the name of dependence on the
Spirit or who engage in little structure and much repetition. I

suggest that it is actually more honouring to God to depend also on the Spirit during diligent preparation; and less honouring to go unprepared and depend upon him only once the saints have gathered. I suggest that repetition of a chorus beyond, say, twice is an assault upon taste and reason. I assume you agree that freedom works both ways: to clap, dance and raise our hands, or not. If you do, would you encourage us to do either with equal liberty and avoid implying to quiet bruisable personalities 'the more clapping and dancing the more liberated and spiritual'? But above all, will you please take us from a suitable start, through a programme based on principles of worship, to a suitable way of concluding? Here are some suggestions.

Worship is a two-direction movement, mediated in both directions by Jesus. Consider the dynamic pendulum movement of a well planned service. Reduced to its essentials it might look something like this:

ORDER OF SERVICE

God Acts		We re-act
HE CALLS	'Come to Me ...'	WE COME
	Opening praise/hymn	PRAISE
	Prayer	INVOKE
SPEAKS	Bible Reading	
	SERMON	LISTEN
	Offering	GIVE
	Prayer	INTERCEDE
	Hymn or Song	DEDICATE
		OURSELVES
	Lord's Supper and hymn?	FEED
		AND RESPOND
SENDS WITH BLESSING		GO TO SERVE

So when a leader says 'Let us worship God!' he isn't saying 'We'll start now', or (as I heard recently) 'This is the summer so we'll just have a short light service.' He or she is directing our minds and hearts to God.

In the opening hymn we aren't climbing out of Saturday late night tiredness; we are giving heart, lung and voice to the praise of God. In the opening prayer the leader's job is to take us, as it were, by the scruff of our necks from inattention to unite and bow our hearts before the majesty and Saviourhood of God; and then speaking for all of us to beg him to shine his light upon and touch us in our need. And so we could go on.

The task of the leader is to consider what each part of the service is doing there and how to make it achieve that. I have said that a service should have shape; I mean that it should be integrated into one harmonious whole: the hymns chosen to support what is preached and chosen also to give the people present - those particular people, with their personal histories, musical preferences and language style - opportunity to express to God what is true of him and how they feel about him, in language that is meaningful for them.

This issue, the shape and structure of worship, raises also the much debated issue of participation. I have already called for space for member-contribution somewhere in the life of a church, not necessarily at the main diet of worship. But what is often asserted, falsely in my view, is that to have only one person up front leading somehow reduces participation ('a monologue to the uncomplaining' is the charge) and to add to the number at the front increases it. This seems to me a misunderstanding.

It was the custom before the Reformation to advise those who came to Mass to say their own private prayers while the incomprehensible Latin rite was carried out away up front. Even a century later the Westminster Directory felt compelled to urge people to attend to the service rather than engage in their own private devotions, reading, 'whispering, conferences, salutations, sleeping and other indecent behaviour'. [9] Now that *is* non-participation. But its opposite is not to have everyone up front, but everyone committed together to the one thing that is going on: listening and responding to the lead, given unitedly to the corporate praise, attending as one people to the preached word in active, eager listening and obedient response. The index of participation is not the number up front but the active involvement of all in solidarity with the leaders, bound up in the bundle of living worship together.

5. The more Joyful, the more Spiritual

Let our final note be joy. 'Come, let us sing for joy to the LORD', said the Psalmist, 'let us shout aloud to the Rock of our salvation. Let us come before him with thanksgiving and extol him with music and song' (Ps. 95:1-2). 'Rejoice in the Lord always', said Paul, 'I will say it again: Rejoice!' The more joyful worship is, the more spiritual: not necessarily happy-clappy, that's a matter of personal style, but committed to glad boasting about God and his Saviourhood, for that is a Christian commandment. It is as God is glorified and enjoyed that we are fulfilled, outsiders attracted and he honoured as he deserves. Such a people will know God's presence, power and pleasure: such a people will be the church at worship.

BIBLIOGRAPHY:
1. Quoted in E J Alexander, St George's Tron Church magazine, summer 1981.
2. D Kidner, *Psalms* (Tyndale Old Testament Commentary) on Psalm 22:3.
3. John Murray, *Collected Writings* Vol.1, Edinburgh, 1976, p.165.
4. E J Alexander, St George's Tron Church magazine, summer 1981.
5. J B Torrance, 'The Place of Jesus Christ in Worship', in Ray S Anderson, ed., *Theological Foundations for Ministry*, Edinburgh, 1979, p.367.
6. John Calvin, *Institutes of the Christian Religion*, 2.6.1.
7. William Still, Gilcomston South Church congregational letter, February 1989.
8. Paul Beasley-Murray, *Dynamic Leadership*, London, 1990, p.146.
9. *Directory for the Public Worship of God*, February 1645.

Chapter 4

And To Teach Its Members
(The Church and Theology)

Geoffrey W Grogan

Rev Geoffrey Grogan is Principal Emeritus of the College. His theological studies were undertaken there and at the London Bible College. He served the College as a full-time lecturer for fourteen years before going south in 1965 to teach at LBC. In 1969 he returned to Glasgow as principal. He has served on four missionary councils, on the Strathclyde Education Committee and the Management Committee for the Cambridge University Diploma in Religious Studies. He has written books on the *Trinity*, the *Person of Christ* and the *Book of Isaiah*. Since retiring in 1990 he has served as part-time Associate Minister of Queens Park Baptist Church in Glasgow and is writing on 'Paul and his Problems' for Christian Focus Publications.

Chapter 4

And To Teach Its Members
(The Church and Theology)

Geoffrey W Grogan

Some readers may have skipped this chapter and come back to it only after reading all the rest! If this is what you did, why did you do it?

Because theology is boring! What a bad image it has even with many Christians! No doubt some theologians have a lot to answer for in this respect. Theology is sometimes expressed in language that is too abstruse and there is little concession to the lay reader. Theologians with a gift for simple exposition of great themes at a level suitable for the general reader are in short supply.

Because theology is arid and spiritually unhelpful! We have to admit there can be some truth in this. If the business of theology is to replace prayer with philosophy, adoration with abstraction, worship with wordiness, and to turn all imperatives into indicatives, then such objections need to be heard. But is this its function?

Is there any deeper theology in the Bible than in Ephesians 1? Yet a glance at verses 3, 6, 12 and 14 will show you that every scrap of it comes to us in a context of praise. Not 'the God and Father of our Lord Jesus Christ has blessed us...' but, 'Blessed be the God and Father of our Lord Jesus Christ, who has blessed us...' The present writer has found the study of theology to be a deeply devotional experience.

Because theology is divisive! It has always set Christians against each other. True or false? Without doubt there is some truth in it. The history of theology is noisy with abusive speech and even with the clash of swords.

Now even the Bible itself uses strong language at times in the interest of good theology. Read Galatians 1 or 2 Peter 2. You see, the Bible writers knew that truth matters, and that serious error can lead to very serious consequences, to personal damnation and the damnation of others who may be influenced by it.

It has to be admitted though that at times theologians have given the impression that every 'i' has to be dotted and every 't' crossed in exactly the same way, making somebody a transgressor for a word. Paul could seem very intolerant when the gospel itself was at stake, but he would not engage in unprofitable disputes about words.

Because theology is irrelevant, God has given us his Word and that is all we need. Yet a study of the Bible makes it abundantly clear that the Bible writers themselves had a theological framework in their minds when they were writing under the inspiration of the Holy Spirit. For one thing, the gospel itself is truth about God, Christ and ourselves, and this gospel is never far away from the thoughts of any of the New Testament writers.

Because theology is simply knowledge that puffs up, not experience that builds up! Of course experience matters and it is only too possible to have a purely intellectual interest in spiritual things. One theologian of the past, recognising this danger, said that it was possible not to believe any more, not to love any more, not to hope any more, but to know what faith and love are, so that all that remains is to assign them their place in the System!

Of course this is a danger to be avoided. It is though vitally important that experience should be authentically Christian, a real encounter with God in Christ. To say that is at once to raise theological questions.

In fact theology is essential to the church. It is certainly not poison to be avoided; it is not even simply medicine for the church's ailments; it is food without which it would starve to death.

1. The Importance of Theology for the Church

There is a tendency today to play down the intellectual aspects of the Christian faith in the interests of experience. It is one thing, however, to say that Christianity is nothing more than right doctrine and quite another to say that doctrine has little to do with it. The possible consequences of such devaluation of theology are very serious indeed.

Consider the following facts:

a. The Basis of the New Testament is Theological

The New Testament contains different types of literature. What is it that unites them all: the Gospels, the Acts of the Apostles, the Epistles and the Book of the Revelation? It is both Christian experience and Christian theology. Remember though that the experience itself is based on the theology, because the Christians had all responded to the preaching of the theological message.

Remember too that the theology is based on history. The history is concerned with Jesus of Nazareth, his life, death, resurrection and ascension. Jesus and the New Testament writers do not simply record the historical facts. They give meaning to them, and that meaning is theological for they explain them in terms of God.

Many writers have demonstrated the essential theological unity of the New Testament books. There have, of course, been attempts to show that the New Testament does not speak with one voice as far as its message is concerned but many of us remain unconvinced.

When Paul says, 'I passed on to you as of first importance that Christ died for our sins according to the Scriptures, that he was buried, that he was raised on the third day according to the Scriptures' (1 Cor 15:3-4), documentation for these words can be found extensively throughout the New Testament literature. The death and resurrection of Jesus are the historical foundation for the gospel of forgiveness in the New Testament.

What the scholars call the *kerygma*, that is the proclamation, the message, is the uniting factor, and everything else in the New Testament presupposes it, emerges from it or is part of its theological context.

To say that Christ died for our sins is to make a statement that is both historical and theological, and the two are bound together. They are also the basis of genuine Christian experience.

b. The New Testament Writers Inherited a Theology from the Old Testament

Jesus did not reject or modify the great truths of the Old Testament although he did challenge the way some Old Testament truths and passages were interpreted in the Judaism of his day.

Actually we can exaggerate even this. The theology of Jesus was in fact remarkably close to that of the Pharisees on almost everything. The nature of the Messiah and how people find acceptance with God are the two main exceptions.

It is sometimes said that the New Testament places such emphasis on Christ that God almost recedes into the background. This is not really true, but any semblance of truth there may be in it is due to the fact that there was no need for the great Old Testament doctrines to be established or ex-

pounded again. They were the living theological heritage of
the men who wrote our New Testament.

c. In Every Age Christianity Exists in a Religious World

The Christian faith was not proclaimed in a vacuum in New
Testament times. It originated, of course, in the Holy Land,
but it soon began to move out into the lands of the Gentiles.
When it arrived there it encountered devotees of many other
religions.

This posed some problems for the preachers. Some of the
Greek terms used in the New Testament in proclaiming the
gospel were also employed in other religious systems in the
world of the day.

In this respect, Paul was God's gift to the infant church.
Although a Jew, he had been born in a Gentile land and was,
therefore, acquainted with many of the thought-forms of first
century paganism. The careful use of these common terms by
a man like Paul, who knew the Old Testament background,
was of great value in this situation.

In some ways the situation is similar in Britain and some
other parts of western Europe today. After a period of many
centuries when most Christians had little contact with people
of other faiths, except perhaps the occasional Jew, once more
various faiths exist side by side. Immigration has brought
people to Britain from many lands, and especially from the
Indian sub-continent where there is such religious pluralism.

Obviously in such a situation Christians must have adequate theological understanding of their faith. Let us not
forget that the church in North Africa was extinguished by the
advance of Islam largely because it did not have the Bible in
the language of the people. Christians there were practically
defenceless against Islam's theological assaults as well as its
physical weaponry.

d. Christianity Also Finds Itself Confronted by Philosophies
The early Christians faced some formidable opposition from
Greek philosophy. They had to out-think their opponents.

In Alexandria the great Neoplatonist philosopher Plotinus
was holding lectures on philosophy at the same time that
Origen was lecturing on Christian theology. Origen found it
important to deal with many of the questions raised by
Plotinus.

It is significant that the most important theologians of the
Middle Ages belonged to orders of friars. These friars had an
evangelistic motivation. They were aware of the philosophical ideas affecting people in the market places and in the new
universities of the time and they had to think through how they
were going to deal with them.

There are, of course, some common areas of interest
between theology and philosophy. Questions about the
existence and nature of God and of spiritual reality, as well as
the nature and destiny of human beings, are some of these.

In fact, as Paul Avis says in his book, *Thresholds of
Theology* (p.2), 'Whenever our thoughts turn to questions of
the meaning of life, ultimate values and the mystery of human
destiny, we are theologising, doing theology.'

The difference between the philosophical and theological
approaches to such questions is largely one of method,
although of course the difference is very important. The
theologian begins from a given religious authority (for the
evangelical Christian of course it is the Bible), whereas the
philosopher does not.

*e. Without Theology Christianity would Dissolve into Relativ-
ism and Individualism*
Until two hundred years ago all Christian theologians started,
as we have said, from a definite authority, and for Protestants

that was always the Bible. In modern times many theologians have tried to dispense, in part at least, with such an authority. This has left a gap, which has often been filled by some philosophy. This means then that philosophy has come to exert a strong influence on theology.

Two largely incompatible principles have, therefore, been contending for the mastery in many modern theologies, the Bible and some philosophy.

In modern times, Protestant theologians have usually been divided into conservatives and liberals. It has been recognised, of course, that the extent to which liberal theologians departed from full Biblical authority has varied considerably.

Don Cupitt, however, distinguishes between conservatives, liberals and radicals and places himself in the last category. He sees liberalism as an unsatisfactory half-way house which must be abandoned. It tries to retain some semblance of supernaturalism, which he reckons is now untenable.

In his book, *Radicals and the Future of the Church*, (p.14), he says, 'Your God has to be, let's be blunt about it, your own personal and temporary improvization...We argue for...pure anarchy...' On page 59, he says, 'The Christian must now be beliefless...Adrift on the open sea of meaning we no longer have any absolute Beginning, End, Foundation, Anchorage or Centre...There is no permanent essence of Christianity, however minimal, because there are no essences.'

The last clause in this quotation shows very clearly that there is a philosophical origin to his thought. In fact it shows that he has surrendered totally to non-Christian philosophy on a matter of the very greatest importance. A few moments' thought will show us that such absolute surrender must lead to individualism. This is because one philosophy will appeal to one theologian and another to another.

Incidentally Cupitt's concept of the church of the future is that it will be a kind of religious club.

2. The Significance of Theology for the Whole Church

If Divine truth, the truth of the gospel, is the basis for the life of the whole church, it follows that good theology ought to permeate it. If this is so then it must be taught to every member. How tragic then that it is often thought of as the special province only of the professional: the minister, the missionary, the religious education teacher!

a. It is Needed by Evangelists

Evangelism is about the spread of the good news and it is particularly concerned with the acceptance of Christ by the individual.

There must be an instructive element in evangelism. If we are to trust Christ we need to know something about him. Nobody can believe in a vacuum but only in a person. The Person Christians believe in has a particular character - he is the Word made flesh - and he has done a particular work for our salvation - dying for our sins and rising again.

It is vital for us to resist any attempt to de-theologise evangelism. In one of his sermons, printed in his book, *The Shaking of the Foundations*, (page 163), Paul Tillich says, 'You are accepted..., accepted by that which is greater than you, and the name of which you do not know. Do not ask for the name now; perhaps you will find it later.' But this is quite contrary to New Testament evangelism. Salvation was offered in a definite name, the name of Jesus.

In fact, a little thought will show that faith always takes its distinctive character from the nature of its object. How can there be true faith unless we know something of the object of our faith?

An experience may be life-changing without being authentically Christian. Shirley MacLaine and other New Age devotees claim to have had life-changing experiences, and yet they are strongly opposed to biblical Christianity.

Evangelism may, of course, be authentically Christian and yet be open to criticism. Some evangelistic messages that present the Christ of the Bible are thin on biblical truth.

What is the least a person needs to know to have an authentic experience of Christ? This may be an interesting and even a useful question, but of, course, we should never be content to present minimum objective content in our preaching. The more our hearers know of Christ the stronger will be the basis for their personal faith when it is exercised.

b. It is Needed by Church-Planters

Both at home and abroad the work of the church-planter is very important. He is an evangelist but he is more. He has to guide small companies composed largely if not entirely of quite new Christians as they seek to establish simple church structures, to appoint leaders and to order the different aspects of developing church life.

In such matters there is always the temptation to adopt a purely pragmatic approach, or perhaps to employ techniques learned in management courses. But the church of Christ is not a business organisation. Its aims and motivation are entirely different.

What folly it would be to attempt such work without a thorough grasp of the New Testament doctrine of the church! A study of the New Testament shows us that Paul wrote some profound theology to some quite new churches. He must have been convinced both that they needed it and that they could take it.

c. It is Needed by Pastors and Preachers

The Christian pastor is by definition a shepherd. A shepherd may do more than provide food for his flock but he can do no less. Peter was told by his Lord to feed his sheep (John 21), and we find that the first Christian converts, brought to Christ through Peter's preaching, were taught apostolic doctrine (Acts 2:42). In his Letters too he teaches Christian truth to the people of God.

The preacher has to understand something of the intellectual atmosphere of the day in which he lives, for this is the atmosphere in which his hearers live their lives. What he needs most however is good theology based on biblical authority.

Julius Wellhausen was a leading Old Testament scholar in Germany during the latter part of the 19th century. His views on the Pentateuch seemed to many to undermine its authority as the Word of God. In a letter to the Prussian Minister of Education, resigning from his professorship, he made a most significant admission:

> I became a theologian because I was interested in the academic study of the Bible. It then gradually dawned on me that a professor of theology also has the practical task of preparing students in the Protestant Church and I was not up to this practical task. Despite every restraint on my part, I was making my pupils more unsuitable for it. Since then, my theological professorship has been a heavy burden on my conscience.

This letter is quoted in John Bowden's chapter in *God's Truth*: Essays to celebrate the 25th Anniversary of 'Honest to God', edited by Eric James (page 50).

Perhaps some theological professors today should weigh those words!

d. It is Needed by Bible Translators

It might seem at first sight that the Bible translator ought to avoid theology like the plague. It has often been pointed out, for instance, that James Moffatt's liberalism seems to have affected his translation from time to time. Anyone well read theologically could be forgiven for concluding that the basic translation work on the Epistle to the Romans in the New English Bible was done by C H Dodd, the chairman of the New Testament panel, for his theology can be clearly seen in it. In the same version the opening of the story of the Tower of Babel in Genesis 11 speaks volumes about the theology of its translator(s), for it reads, 'Once upon a time...'!

Nevertheless the translator does need theology, good biblical theology. A biblical word or phrase, taken out of context, may have more than one possible meaning. When read in its context, the intended meaning often becomes clear. Where it does not, then it is important to relate it to the teaching of that biblical author elsewhere, and if all else fails to take its meaning from the general teaching of Scripture. The last two processes certainly require theology.

e. It is Needed by Leaders of the Local Church

Most churches have a plurality of leaders. There may be a minister, there may be elders and/or deacons or their equivalents. There will probably be a secretary and a treasurer. Probably only a proportion of these will have a teaching gift, but some theological understanding is needed by them as a group. Important decisions affecting a whole local church are often made by such Christian people. It is vitally important that these should be made in a way consistent with the faith once for all delivered to the saints.

For instance, the treasurer, who will have responsibility for making recommendations about the use of the church's income, will need to understand what, according to New Testament teaching, are the main values a local church should recognise and the main activities it should have. These will then determine its financial priorities.

Many of these people will be involved in pastoral visitation. Church members, especially those watching others suffer, are likely to ask some deep questions, questions that are really theological. They have a right to expect leaders of the church to be able to give them some help from the Scriptures.

f. It is Needed by Students

We are not referring simply to theological students here but to all who are undergoing academic study. In fact, much that will be said here applies also to school pupils, especially in some subjects and particularly at the higher levels.

In so many academic disciplines, there are certain assumptions which are widely accepted, but which in fact conflict with Christian truth. This is particularly true when assumptions are made about the nature of human beings. General convictions about the nature of human life affect subjects like biology, psychology, sociology, economics, medicine, law, criminology and many others.

It is to be feared that many Christian students pursue a kind of 'double-think'. They keep their Christian faith and their academic studies in separate compartments. Ultimately this can be destructive either of faith or of personal integrity or both. Students need some theological preparation if they are to face the deeper questions which emerge from their academic studies.

g. It is Needed by Every Christian

If the Christian life begins when we get to know the truth of Christ, and the Holy Spirit uses this truth to bring us to personal faith in him, it is nourished by continual appropriation of that truth.

Jesus said that it was those who continued in his Word who were truly his disciples. He said that they would know the truth and the truth would set them free (John 8:30-32). So truth and freedom are not enemies but friends.

Certainly the intellectual nature of the Christian faith can be over-emphasised but it can also be underplayed. The Christian's developing experience of the Christ of faith is mediated through biblical truth.

Now there may be some who would accept what we have been saying in the last few paragraphs and yet who would still dispute the 'ordinary' Christian's need for theology, maintaining that all he or she needs is constant exposure to the Bible itself.

Much as we may sympathise with this outlook, we must assert that it is mistaken. God has given us minds. Even Christians who know nothing about formal theology nevertheless have a system of beliefs, more or less articulate, in their minds. If this is so, then it is surely important for these beliefs to be tested, refined and expanded by good teaching which will give a balanced presentation of the whole range of biblical truth!

If we are to give 'a reason for the hope that is in us,' this implies a thoughtful reply on the basis of at least a rudimentary theological understanding of the Christian's hope in Christ.

3. Christian Theology and Other Systems of Thought

Throughout its history, the Christian gospel has always gone out into a world full of conflicting voices, often at odds not only with the gospel but also with each other. This has presented it with problems but also with opportunities.

a. The Theology of our Gospel has to be both Biblically Authentic and Culturally Relevant

In Acts 17, we see Paul in his encounter with Epicurean philosophers in Athens. If we examine his address on that occasion, as B Gartner and others have shown, we notice two important facts.

Firstly, his message engaged with the ideas of both Stoics and Epicureans, confirming truth and combating error. If he declared, 'As some of your own poets have said...' he also said, 'The God who made the world and everything in it...does not live in temples built by hands.'

Secondly, his message never lost contact with the Old Testament roots of the gospel. Although he never quoted the Old Testament on that occasion, because the people knew nothing of it, his message is saturated with its language and ideas.

In itself the biblical gospel was retained in all its purity while it was applied in such a way as to challenge the world-view of the hearers.

Paul's example has not always been followed. Sometimes Christians have retreated into theological isolationism. At other times they have had dialogue with alien systems of thought in such a way that they have not simply employed the language of philosophy but have absorbed philosophical ideas into the very substance of their theology.

This can be seen, for instance, in systems of thought as widely scattered in Christian history as early Gnosticism, mediaeval Albigensianism and the modern 'Death of God' theology.

The challenge, therefore, for the Christian theologian is to provide a basis for preaching the gospel in terms that are culturally relevant to his society and yet at the same time without loss or contamination of biblical content. This is a demanding and highly responsible task, but is both necessary and rewarding. There is undoubtedly an intellectual side to conversion. This is emphasised in the apologetic method advocated by Cornelius Van Til. In this, the unbeliever is confronted with the truth. He has to repent of his outlook as well as of his lifestyle and he needs to begin to learn God's truth with the attitude of a little child, sitting at the feet of Jesus.

In order to gain the ear of the unbeliever, however, we need to use language he can understand but fill it with authentic gospel content.

b. It Needs to be Relevant to the Western World

In his work, *The Two Cultures*, written in 1959, C P Snow dealt with the scientific and artistic casts of mind and with the way western education both expressed and promoted their divergence. He was concerned that the gap should be bridged and particularly that those who belonged to the artistic culture should become better acquainted with the world of the sciences.

Five years later, Arthur Koestler wrote, *The Act of Creation*. In this he demonstrated that the birth of scientific theories and the creation of works of art have important features in common. In all the interest today in the diverse functions of the left and right sides of the brain this should not be forgotten.

What is true is that theological education in the west has related much more thoroughly to artistic than to scientific culture. Many ministers have an arts degree, but how few have had a scientific education to Honours Degree level! We need many more science graduates whose theological education has been of such a kind that they can preach the gospel in a way that relates to western scientific man. Perhaps somebody reading these words may hear in them a call from God.

Neither should we forget the social and behavioural sciences. They are all concerned with areas in which Christians should take a real interest. Often they are taught with philosophical assumptions which are rationalistic and humanistic, and the sad thing is that many Christian students may not even realise that this is the case.

We dare not promote the kind of 'double-think' we noted above. We need theologians who are able to relate the gospel to the worlds of psychology, sociology and economics.

c. It Needs to be Relevant to the Post-Communist World

At the present time, world communism is in retreat and many countries are moving away from a communist ideology. This requires reorientation not only in terms of politics, economics and philosophy, but in many other aspects of culture.

It is very important for theologians and preachers to be sensitive to this new situation. Those who have been reared within a communist ideological system necessarily think differently from those whose thinking is conditioned, whether they realise it or not, by western philosophies.

Certainly the two worlds have never been completely separate intellectually. The most dominant philosophy in the west for some time after the Second World War was Existentialism. In fact both Existentialism and Marxism were reactions against the philosophy of Hegel that was so influential in the 19th century. This means that they could not help having some features in common. This is true also of Logical Positivism which had a period of influence some decades ago, especially in scientific circles.

Nevertheless with all the similarities, there are profound differences. These need to be studied.

A post-communist society crying out for authentic truth

must be fed. At a time when many churches in these countries
are at last free to establish places of theological training for
their pastors, it is vital that those who come from the west to
help them in this task should have considerable cultural
sensitivity as well as being completely faithful to the Biblical
gospel.

d. It Needs to be Relevant to the 'Third World'

This term, self-chosen by the non-aligned nations during the
opening months of the Cold War, becomes increasingly
inappropriate as retreat from communism reduces the gap
between the other two worlds.

It has, however, come to have economic as well as political
connotations and for this reason it may survive for some time
yet. It is usually applied to the nations of Asia, Africa and
Latin America, although even in its economic sense it is no
longer applicable to Japan, Saudi Arabia and some other
nations.

By it we mean the nations of these three areas, where other
factors beside those coming from western civilisation have
had a major effect on the culture of the people. This is, of
course, more marked in some places than others, as a comparison, for instance, of the urban areas of Brazil with rural Tibet,
or even with the interior of Brazil itself, would quickly show.

Western theologians have tended to be insular. Quite
understandably they have developed their theologies in the
context of the intellectual climate of the western world. There
is nothing wrong with this. In fact, to fail to do this would itself
have been reprehensible.

Unfortunately, however, some have tended to think this
the only way to do theology. They have never come to terms
with the need for the development of Christian theologies that
are relevant to particular Third World cultures.

William Dyrness, in his book, *Learning about Theology from the Third World*, written in 1990, makes an interesting observation when he says that African theologians want particularly to relate theology to various cultures, while those from Latin America are interested in its political implications and Asian theologians are concerned to relate their faith to the religious values of the major religions of that continent.

There is truth in this generalisation although it is, of course, more a matter of particular emphasis than of exclusive preoccupation.

It is very important for western theologians to seek dialogue with their colleagues whose background is in quite different cultures. Dyrness also points out that Third World theologies need to grapple more than they have so far with the fact of modernization which is, of course, making an impact on their cultures.

There is no doubt that Liberation Theology, especially the Latin American variety, has had considerable influence on recent western theology. The insistence of Liberation theologians that theology is not purely an abstract study, but that it can only be properly pursued by people with a commitment to the poor and oppressed, has much to teach us.

Too often we have separated doctrine and life. The refusal to do this is one of the virtues of Oliver Barclay's book, *Developing a Christian Mind*. In it he emphasises the essentially practical bearing of a truly Christian theology.

In fact, the editors and authors of *Paradigm Change in Theology*, published in 1989, are convinced that, in the words of Hans Kung (p.4), 'one theological 'paradigm', or model of understanding, is being replaced by another' and that theologians need to come to terms with this.

It is Liberation Theology and its predecessor, Theology of Hope, that have made this paradigm change seem necessary to many theologians, with their emphasis on practical commitment and not simply intellectual understanding.

If there is any truth in this, it shows that at last a theological current is to be seen running towards rather than away from Europe, although, of course, we still have to ask the question as to how much Liberation Theology owes to Marxism which originated, of course, in Europe.

4. Urgent Tasks Facing Christian Theology

These become more and more numerous and more and more urgent every year. There will be no space to do more than make a few suggestions, and then only in three doctrines.

1. The Doctrine of Creation

There are all sorts of current issues here. How is theology to relate to the shifting paradigms in science, and to recent developments in cosmology? The whole ecological area of things needs to be addressed much more fully than we have done so far.

The supernatural dimension of the created universe now holds fascination for those who have experienced the bankruptcy of materialism. Not only in animistic societies but in western countries there is an increasing belief in a spiritual dimension within the physical world. Much of this interest is anything but Christian, but it compels us to ask ourselves what theology of the supernatural we have?

2. The Doctrine of Humanity

This doctrine has often been conceived much too narrowly.

What does the Bible have to say, for instance, about the child and the foetus? What is the value of old age and what is the significance of death? Is there a theology of race in the Bible? What about all the feminist issues? Is there a theological guide to light our way in the sexual confusion of today?

What theology of society can be gained from Scripture and does this have political implications? Questions of a social nature are endless.

How, in the light of the doctrine of humanity, are Christians to view the arts, the natural sciences, the social sciences?

3. The Doctrine of Scripture
The whole debate in modern times about knowledge and communication needs to be thought through theologically.

What are the forms in which God's truth comes to us in the Bible? Does inspiration work in the same way in all the varied literary genre in Scripture? What place is there for symbol and metaphor? What about acted prophecy?

Those who are interested in the structure of literature and the way this reflects structures in the human mind are raising important questions. Does the Bible have fixed meaning or does it have different meaning for each reader according to the impact it makes on his or her mind? The way we answer this question is obviously very important for the authority of the Bible.

These are but a few of the many questions that call for urgent attention.

Chapter 5

For Christian Ministry
(The Church and the Ministry)

Derek Prime

Rev Derek Prime read history and theology at Cambridge. After some teaching experience, he was called in 1957 to the pastorate of Lansdowne Evangelical Free Church in South London. In the year 1966/67 he was President of the Fellowship of Independent Evangelical Churches. In 1969 he commenced a long pastorate at Charlotte Chapel, Edinburgh. In 1987 he resigned to concentrate on itinerant ministry and writing. He also gave a year to part-time lecturing at the College. He has written many books and has a gift for showing the practical application of Biblical teaching. He has written much for Christian Focus Publications, including a series explaining Christian doctrine to children.

Chapter 5

For Christian Ministry
(The Church and the Ministry)

Derek Prime

'You are taking up a far nobler calling.' That comment was made to me in the mid-fifties when I shared my decision to leave school-teaching for the ministry. I doubt whether many would feel that way today. A hundred years ago - and much less - people needing help would have gone to a minister. Today they may go instead to their doctor, a counsellor or a psychiatrist. The contemporary caricature of a minister depicts him as largely irrelevant to real life, and something of an oddity.

Within the church itself, there have also been radical changes in the manner in which it views its ministers. Churches which have traditionally held to the concept of what is called somewhat disparagingly 'a one-man ministry' now favour shared and team ministry. Churches which throughout their history have abhorred the idea of ever having a pastor - or a leader among leaders - have come to recognise the need for some such leadership.

Ministers themselves in many parts of the church find they have something of an identity crisis. Whereas a few decades ago their job description was straightforward, both charismatic renewal and the house-church movement have brought into question some of their traditional duties. Once they might have been regarded as indispensable, but now they may even be likened to corks in bottles - hindrances to the gifts and ministry of others.

It is much more difficult to be a minister or pastor today than it was thirty years ago, and this must have some bearing on the tragic leakage of personnel from the ministry, often after only a short time, and sometimes after many years. The somewhat violent winds of change which have blown through the church have made it difficult to hold people together, although the burden for trying to maintain unity inevitably rests upon the minister.

The backgrounds from which we come inevitably colour our thinking about the ministry. We have in view in this chapter those who fulfil the New Testament calling of 'pastors and teachers' (Eph. 4:11). The two terms denote the same office, and shepherding and teaching are twin tasks.

Church history, right up to the present, demonstrates that our Lord Jesus Christ raises up such people. Individual churches may use different names for 'pastors and teachers' but that is essentially what they are. Not all may give their full time to the task, but that is not the crucial criterion. The all-important qualification is Christ's call.

How the Church should View its Ministers

1. Ministers Should be Viewed as Christ's Gift

Churches do not create or give rise to ministers - the Holy Spirit does this (Acts 20:28). From the beginning the emphasis has been upon God's choice, not that of his people (Deut. 21:5). While churches have the duty of recognising a person's call, they are not its source. God calls and qualifies those whom he calls (2 Cor. 3:6).

Ministers are pre-eminently 'ministers of Jesus Christ' (Rom. 15:16; Col. 1:7; 1 Tim. 4:6). Their calling, gifting and job description is from him, and their sole duty is to please him. They are not to look for their primary encouragement from success or people but from the great privilege of their calling (2 Cor. 4:1). While they know themselves to be like common earthenware jars, they are to have a high view of the ministry because of the treasure entrusted to them (2 Cor. 4:7; Rom. 11:13). No one who enters the ministry should think of it in terms of sacrifice: it is the highest honour. As Christ's gift, ministers are to be held in respect by the church on account of the work they do and the office they hold (1 Thess. 5:12-13).

2. Ministers Should be seen as Simply God's Servants

The New Testament knows nothing of a priestly caste; rather it proclaims the priesthood of all believers. Whatever views we have of the ministry they must never be in conflict with the spiritual priesthood of the whole church. The minister must not be thought of in terms which neglect the fact that the church is a society of equals.

The passage of time has sadly obscured the truth that 'ministry' means service. The New Testament word is *diakonia* from which we get our word 'deacon'. Above everything else that the minister is, he is a servant (1 Cor. 3:5-9). Moses, David, Daniel and Paul, together with many others, regarded this as their most appropriate self-description. All who serve the best interests of the body of Christ walk in the footsteps of him who was uniquely the Servant of the Lord.

The minister's task is to provide a model for God's people to follow (1 Cor. 11:1; Phil. 4:8-9), since every Christian should aspire to be a servant of Christ.

3. Ministers Should be seen as Elders Among Elders

The pastor or minister is one of the elders of the church, although the term 'elder' may not be used by every local church fellowship. Pastors often function as the principal teaching elders and the presiding elders, although it is custom and convenience rather than biblical direction that makes this the case. The reason is that while their fellow elders share their calling, they have not been set aside to give the whole of their time to the work. The proper pastoral care of the flock, and the provision of spiritual pasture for them through the ministry of God's Word, demands that one or more of their number be set apart for this task to a greater degree than others.

4. Ministers Should be Expected to Lead

God's people require leadership. We must not be afraid of leadership as if it were somehow or other not really Christian to want to lead. Christian leadership models itself upon our Lord Jesus Christ. One of the paradoxes of his ministry was that although he was so obviously the Leader, he was conspicuously the Servant.

We must reinstate in the thinking of God's people 'the trust-worthy saying' of the early church: 'If anyone sets his heart on being an overseer, he desires a noble task' (1 Tim. 3:1). Those who are called to minister will have a God-given desire to lead God's people forward, and will be gifted to do so. Paul's exhortation in Romans 12 that if an individual's gift is leadership he should 'govern diligently' (verse 8) implies the temptation to shrink sometimes from the exercise of leadership because of its demanding nature.

When God's people are in danger of fragmentation because of divisive views on secondary issues, ministers in particular must stir themselves up to give a lead in showing the pre-eminence of our Lord Jesus Christ, and the priority of love and unity in his body, the church. If they do not do it, who will?

5. Ministers Themselves Should be Objects of Pastoral Care

There is always the danger of putting ministers upon a pedestal and of forgetting that they too need those who will be watchful for their spiritual well-being. Denominations often try to make provision for this, although not always successfully.

The best provision is within the local churches themselves, where the other spiritual leaders delegate some of their number to feel particular spiritual responsibility for their pastors and their families. Ministers should be quick to acknowledge their need of this, and make it easy for the people to whom this task is delegated to exercise it. To push aside such spiritual care is tantamount to suggesting that the need does not exist - and that attitude inevitably preludes a fall.

How Ministers should see the
Outworking of their Calling

1. Prayer
When the apostles instituted the appointment of what were probably the first 'deacons' (Acts 6:1ff.) the apostles' God-inspired intention was to give themselves to prayer and the ministry of the Word (Acts 6:4). The latter is easier than the former.

The apostles were modelling themselves - perhaps unconsciously - upon their Master's example. No one was busier than he, or surrounded more by the demands of people, but the daily priority of his life was his time alone with his Father. Each decision and important change of direction in his ministry followed his seeking his Father's face. He taught them that certain blessings would come only as they gave themselves seriously to prayer.

If no one else prays for every member of their congregations by name, ministers should. If no one else prays through every item on the agenda for elders' and deacons' meetings, pastors should. If no one else asks, 'What would God have us seek from him as a church and congregation?' pastors should.

Ministers' public prayers unconsciously influence the manner God's people pray. For good or ill, they are teaching them by example, and they must determine that it will be a good example. At its best their ministry will be bathed in prayer, and they will have prayed God's truth home in their own lives before they share it with Christ's flock.

2. Teach God's Word

Ministers' principal task, along with prayer, is to give themselves to the Word of God. If they do not do this, they are like workmen who go about their work without their essential tools. They must study the Scriptures so that they are competent to teach 'the whole will of God' (Acts 20:27).

Ministers are to confirm God's people in their understanding of gospel truth (1 Cor. 15:1ff.) and at the same time show them the holiness of life that this truth demands (1 Thess. 4:1ff.). They are to enlarge the members of the flock's understanding of the faith so that they may render a better obedience to our Lord Jesus Christ (Rom. 1:5). Ministers must not lose sight of their calling as the friends of the bride of Christ, the church, to be preparing her for the Bridegroom by constantly showing her the wonders of his Person and work on her behalf.

Expository preaching is one of the key secrets of a ministry of lasting usefulness, but it requires much discipline and hard work to achieve. Behind one half-hour address given to the flock there may be many hours of diligent study and wrestling to convey God's truth with clarity. The local church must ensure that those who are set apart for this ministry are encouraged to give it priority, and not to allow themselves to be side-tracked by what may be permissible - yet not beneficial - competing activities.

3. To Present Everyone Perfect in Christ

Feeding God's people and proclaiming the whole counsel of God are not ends in themselves. They serve a greater end - the goal of presenting every Christian mature in Christ. Paul shared this great objective when he described the essence of his ministry in his Colossian letter: 'We proclaim him (Christ), admonishing and teaching everyone with all wisdom, so that we may present everyone perfect in Christ.' ' To this end,' he continued, 'I labour, struggling with all his energy, which so powerfully works in me' (1:28-29).

A goal of the ministry is the holiness and unreserved obedience to the Lord Jesus Christ of every believer. The public teaching of God's Word, in the context of the church coming together for instruction, must be supplemented and underlined by ministers' use of God's Word in all their contacts with the flock.

Young Christians need early instruction in the first principles of the Christian life. Newly married couples, setting up home, and establishing families, require thoughtful instruction from the Scriptures as to the way they should think and plan their lives. Those who suffer through illness or bereavement want sensitive counsel from the Scriptures as to how they should submit themselves to God in faith and well-doing.

The local church should see its minister as a shepherd whose main concern must be to lead them into the pastures of God's Word appropriate to them at the time. They must also expect their pastor to give priority to the needs of the 'lambs', and the straying sheep.

4. To Prepare God's People for Ministry

An unfortunate aspect of the use of the term 'the ministry' to describe the work of pastors and teachers is that it tends to obscure the fact that the ministry is the ministry of the whole church. The gifts pastors and teachers possess have sometimes been so magnified in the church, that the development of other gifts has been neglected. While the church requires the gift of shepherds and teachers, it equally needs all the other gifts Christ gives to his body. Shepherds' and teachers' particular responsibility is to prepare God's people for their individual works of service (Eph. 4:12). They are to help Christians first to discern their gifts, and then to use them.

This should not be a haphazard exercise but a deliberate one. As they pray for church members by name in daily rotation, they should ask for God's help in identifying each member's gift or gifts, and for pastoral wisdom to encourage their use if their employment is not already plain.

As leaders among leaders, they must ensure that the development and recognition of spiritual gifts within the local church is regularly on the agenda of their meetings. It takes discipline to ask at regular intervals, 'Are there gifts God is giving to members of our church fellowship which we need to recognise and encourage?' but it is a necessary discipline if the subject is not to be pushed to the background because of preoccupation with other more urgent but not more important issues.

5. To Equip God's People for Evangelism

Ministers are always to keep before their congregations their evangelistic responsibility in view of the profound truth that God desires all men and women to be saved, and to come to a knowledge of the truth (1 Tim. 2:3,4). The church is not only to be concerned for its spiritual maturity, but also for its growth. True pastors are concerned for the other sheep who have not yet heard the Great Shepherd's call (John 10:16). The church is healthy as, through the works of service her members are equipped to fulfil, she reaches out into the world

and obeys her Head's final commission to preach the good
news to every creature.

Ministers are to have as a clear goal the equipping of God's
people to be fishers of men and women. They best do this by
example. Besides striving to do the work of an evangelist as
they themselves preach evangelistically, they must personally show a spiritual concern for unconverted neighbours and
friends, and those whom God brings across their path. When
they then urge others to be concerned, their plea will have the
undeniable ring of reality.

Regular, although infrequent courses of instruction in
evangelism within the framework of the church's programme
of teaching have their place, but the emphasis should not be
placed here. Nothing excels the effectiveness of Christians
living out the Christian life wherever God has placed them in
such a telling and attractive manner that people are compelled
to ask them to give the reason for the hope that they have (1
Peter 3:15). Well taught in the Scriptures by pastors and
teachers, they will be able to share the gospel in a way that is
natural and winsome.

All of these ministerial goals are interrelated. As God's
people have the whole of the Scriptures opened up to them,
they discover their responsibility for evangelism. As they are
brought to spiritual maturity, their light becomes brighter and
their saltiness greater, and they thus increase their readiness
for witness.

The Priority of Godliness of Character

Godliness sounds an old-fashioned word, but none can ad-
equately replace it. A godly person does what is right in God's
sight, and does it with an eye to God's praise alone, so that
there is the same standard for what is said, thought or done in
private as in public. Churches seldom, if ever, rise above the

spirituality of their leaders. Ministers, therefore, are to be godly (1 Tim. 6:11).

Robert Murray McCheyne - the godly Dundee minister who died so young - made two most telling statements about a minister's personal life: first, 'My people's greatest need is my personal holiness:' and, second, 'How awful a weapon in the hand of God is a holy minister.'

It is no accident that the New Testament places as great a stress upon character as a qualification for spiritual leadership as upon gift (1 Tim. 3:1-13; Titus 1:6-9). The fruit of the Spirit is as important as the gifts of the Spirit in the life of a pastor and teacher, as in any Christian. No rivalry exists between the two: both are important and necessary. But the gifts of the Spirit cannot be exercised in a God-glorifying manner if the character of the user of the gift is not also God-glorifying (1 Peter 4:7-11).

Whatever else ministers give to God's people, they are to give them an example to follow. James warns against becoming a teacher without due thought 'because we know that we who teach will be judged more strictly' (3:1) - that is to say, according to how far we have been examples of what we ourselves have taught. Peter teaches that elders' principal task is to be 'examples to the flock' (1 Peter 5:3). Only then may they anticipate receiving 'the crown of glory that will never fade away' (1 Peter 5:4). Ministers - whatever their age - are to be like parents providing a good example of love, faith and purity (1 Cor. 11:1). Good examples are part of God's provision to help his people obey the gospel's message (2 Thess. 3:6-7).

While the world at large appears to ignore the value of the church's ministers, it certainly chooses not to ignore any misdemeanours which are brought to its notice. The unconverted may try to find an excuse for not believing the gospel on account of the behaviour of ministers. The apostolic standard, therefore, must be that of pastors: 'We put no stumbling-block in anyone's path, so that our ministry will not be discredited' (2 Cor. 6:3). Ministers have a greater obligation to exemplify godliness because of the public responsibilities they exercise. John Brown's prayer that 'I may not tear God's Church, mangle his truths, betray his honour, or murder the souls of men' is just as relevant in the twentieth century as it was in the eighteenth.

Greater care than ever is required in this matter of example because of the moral and social atmosphere in which we live. A decline in sexual morality and an unhelpful casualness in relationships between the sexes means that ministers must be especially watchful about relationships with those of the opposite sex. If they are wise, they will maintain all proper priorities, and carefully erect barriers against some of the perils to which they may find themselves vulnerable by the very nature of their involvement with people. Church fellowships should not be surprised or resentful of the safeguards they erect, but rather be glad that they recognise their vulnerability and set a high standard.

The ministry any pastors exercise is only effective as it arises from the consecration of their whole life to God. To take care of the flock, ministers must first take care of themselves spiritually and morally (Acts 20:28). If pastors turn aside from the way, they cause many to stumble (Malachi 2:8). When a big tree falls, lots of little trees fall with it. Faithfulness remains a key requirement of ministers (Col. 1:7; 4:7; I Tim. 4:6).

The Church's Training and Equipping of Ministers

Emphases in training change, and our approach to this subject is necessarily determined by how much we are guided by the biblical objectives of the ministry we have stated, and how far we are influenced by contemporary trends which tend to stress 'felt-needs'.

Most denominations provide their own theological colleges, and these have the advantage of focusing particularly upon ministerial training. Some interdenominational colleges also provide training for the ministry, but their focus may not concentrate so much on the work of pastors and teachers because they have other spheres of service in view. Exclusively evangelical seminaries also exist with no denominational allegiance. A very small minority train for the ministry as they actually do the work of a pastor or an assistant in a local church.

Experience proves that God graciously uses all of these and it is important not to be dogmatic about the best means of instructing and equipping pastors, especially as much depends upon their hearts and attitude no matter what form of training they receive.

Nevertheless, there are certain basic principles whatever preparation is given. First, any professed call to the ministry should be tested and, if possible, proved before training is undertaken. The local church has a vital part to play here as the proving ground for an individual's call. If the local church is not wholehearted in endorsing a call - providing, of course, that it is a spiritual company of God's people - no training establishment ought to consider accepting that person, much as they will be understandably concerned to gain sufficient students to make themselves financially viable. No system of proving people's call beforehand is infallible, but we should strive our hardest to avoid mistakes, since not only are the individuals themselves hurt but the church also.

Second, a primary concern of all systems of training must be the development of effective preachers and pastors. Whatever the curriculum, the end of all academic study of theology and of the Scriptures must be to make pastors and teachers as useful as they can possibly be in the communication of God's Word and in the spiritual care of his people. Those who are best equipped to teach theology may not be the best equipped to produce preachers and pastors. Most training establishments will gain much by supplementing their essential full-time staff with the occasional yet regular help of those who are actually engaged in daily pastoring and teaching.

Third, the church needs to make provision for assistantships. This arrangement is available throughout Anglicanism, and frequently in Presbyterianism, but seldom in non-conformity. Sometimes an assistantship is possible during the initial period of training, but more than this is required.

Too many small churches have a record of short pastorates with younger pastors beginning their ministries with them. Small churches are frequently much more difficult to pastor than large churches, and yet that seems to be the context in which so many begin. Inevitably they make their initial mistakes there, and then find themselves inclined to move on at the first opportunity in order to make a fresh start. Most of the problems of first charges would be avoided if more assistantships were available.

Assistantships provide opportunities to observe experienced pastors at work. As assistants are given opportunity to teach and preach, and to engage in pastoral work, their rough edges can be discerned and smoothed out by a more experienced colleague. Mistakes made as assistants will seldom be as disastrous as they would be in a first pastorate without that previous assistantship.

Most important of all, they will gain experience of church leaders' meetings. Few entering the ministry will have had the opportunity of becoming elders or deacons - or the equivalent

- in their home churches, and yet they are expected immediately upon their ordination to chair such meetings. To learn by observation how these meetings should be properly conducted and handled is worth any number of college lectures.

So often local churches may consider the appointment of an assistant purely from their own point of view, asking, in effect, 'What will we gain from calling an assistant?' I would suggest that this is the wrong way round. The primary purpose is to provide the best training and experience for new pastors, and to see this provision - costly as it may be financially - as a contribution to the well-being of the whole body of Christ. As the church seeks to act unselfishly in making this possible, it will inevitably gain, and often in surprising ways. Here as elsewhere, in giving we find ourselves receiving. As we do our best to help young pastors, we will also find ourselves gaining the best from them.

It is vitally important that ministers who have responsibility for assistants should establish the principle of honest appraisal from the beginning of the relationship. Every sermon preached should be reviewed, as should the different aspects of their leadership of the public worship of God's people. Any fault, eccentricity, unhelpful mannerism or habit should be honestly discussed, otherwise they are likely to increase and be perpetuated throughout a minister's career. But dealt with at this early stage, they may be corrected and immeasurable improvement effected. If more purposeful assistantships are provided, first pastorates will not be so short, and sometimes disastrous.

The Practicalities of Support and Housing

The support of the ministry is important because of the teaching of Scripture. The teaching is seldom emphasised from the pulpit because those who might be expected to teach it find it difficult to do so out of a rightful fear of drawing attention to themselves.

Ministers of our Lord Jesus Christ worthy of the name will never want to be influenced by salary or financial considerations in answering God's call to a church. They will certainly not want to be involved in discussions concerning their salary as it may be reviewed from time to time. But that natural and understandable reluctance does not remove from the church its responsibility to care keenly about the material well-being of those who serve it as pastors and teachers.

Those who preach the gospel should receive their living from the gospel - this is the Lord's command (1 Cor. 9:14). Having sown spiritual seed, the New Testament argues, those who minister are to reap also a material harvest (1 Cor. 9:11). Ministers are to be supported financially by those who are instructed by them (Gal. 6:6), for, as our Lord said, 'The worker deserves his wages' (Luke 10:7). Now, I would not expect ministers to say this, or even to expect it. In fact, there may be times when they deliberately choose to forgo their rights in order to further the gospel (1 Cor. 9:12, 15ff.). But that does not absolve the church of its responsibility, and of its necessary obedience to the Word of Christ.

To fix an appropriate salary is often difficult, and it ought plainly to be compatible with the circumstances of fellow-Christians in the local church. One possible approach is to take the mean of the salaries of those sharing in the leadership of the church - whether of the elders or the deacons - so that the pastor's salary would be neither the smallest nor the largest. Another helpful approach is to take some external standard, such as the scale of remuneration of school-teachers, and use this as a constantly updated guide. Whatever method is employed, an annual review of salaries is essential so that the subject is not overlooked. For ministers themselves to be preoccupied with the subject is unspiritual. For the church to neglect it and to regard it as of little importance is equally unspiritual. To support Christ's servants is to give to the Lord Jesus Christ himself. In loving them, they love him.

Churches need to take a serious look at the manner in which ministers are housed. Traditionally they have lived in tied houses - vicarages, rectories and manses. Such an arrangement has plain benefits: the church has a financial asset which can only increase in value, and the church can frequently provide a better family house than the pastor could hope to provide.

But there are disadvantages in that most churches find it difficult to maintain property well, and few homes are universally suitable for the differing needs of the ministers who may be called to live in them. So far as ministers are concerned, they do not have the happy and secure feeling that comes from living with their family in their own place, and they will often feel restricted in the alterations and improvements they would like to make. When retirement comes - or worse still, the premature death of the minister - the family has nowhere to go, and the continued occupation of the church house becomes a mutual embarrassment.

Each situation is unique, and dogmatism must be avoided. Sometimes the ideal arrangement is the payment of an appropriate and realistic salary so that ministers are in a position to buy a house on the open market like many others. A better arrangement sometimes is the shared ownership of the church house. This gives ministers and their families a helpful stake in the property market, the best use of their savings, and the avoidance of embarrassment if sudden bereavement occurs. But identification with the congregation is of fundamental importance, so that if the majority of the congregation live in rented accommodation, there may be a very good argument for ministers and their families living in similar accommodation. Whatever is the outcome, the subject needs to be honestly and realistically discussed, but never to the point where it becomes too important.

Women's Ministry

Women's ministry is a question of contemporary debate. It is not within the scope of this chapter to attempt to deal with it. But the issue is not going to disappear. So far as I can discern, the question is not whether or not women should be ordained or be able to celebrate the Lord's Supper - two major preoccupations of many whenever the subject is raised - but whether or not the Scriptures teach that women should exercise the two principal duties of elders of ruling and teaching.

The straightforward reading of the Scriptures points clearly to these tasks being assigned to men. The apostle Paul's statements are crucial and a variety of interpretations are current. Many arguments are advanced to suggest that either Paul did not mean what his words seem to imply or that he was simply writing as a man of his day. What hinders me from feeling happy about such suggestions is that each time Paul raises the subject he deliberately goes back to Genesis and God's purposes in creation. This undeniable factor seems to undermine any suggestion that he simply wrote as a man of his time.

My principal concern, however, is that the subject should not be divisive. Important as it is, it is not an issue that should separate Christians from one another. When we discuss the subject we must work hard at understanding the Scriptures - and not compromising their authority - rather than aiming to satisfy feminist demands or those who oppose men. We must be willing to accept one another where we differ on the subject, and be honest with each other where different views of ministry may sometimes make co-operation between churches difficult.

Help for Ministers

True pastors are always on call. They tend to live on the job. The crises of the flock will be unexpected and demanding. It is essential that provision is made for them by churches so that these demands do not become too great, and so that they are given space and time to be refreshed and renewed.

The first priority is a regular day off. Churches ought to insist that their pastors take their 'sabbath', and they should fence it as best they can from interruptions. Burn-out has become a contemporary term to describe many pastors' experience, and one root cause of it is the failure to stop - and to stop at least once a week. Emergencies and funerals will inevitably interrupt and sometimes take up completely a day-off. Churches will help their pastors by telling them that they must, if possible, take off time in lieu, and that they are not to have a guilty conscience about doing so.

The second help is annual attendance at a pastors' conference of some sort where they can mix with other pastors, find refreshment for their own souls and spirits, sharpen their minds through conversation with others facing the same spiritual battles and challenges, and stand back and see their own work in a better perspective. If churches would say to their pastors, 'We expect you to go away to a pastors' conference once a year and we want to pay the expenses' they would reap considerable benefits through enriched ministries. I mention the paying of the expenses because so often the cost of going away will be a major hindrance to some.

The third boon is a sabbatical. I only took two sabbaticals in thirty years, but looking back both I and the two churches

I served would doubtless have gained if I had seized the opportunity more frequently. They were times of recharging my batteries, and of fruitful study of the Scriptures. They served too to teach me that my presence was not indispensable. Standing at a distance, and sampling other church fellowships during those periods, I saw my own situation more clearly, and returned with renewed zeal and vision.

While these helps are areas where pastors may need to take some personal initiative, they are most beneficially achieved where churches recognise their importance and insist that they should be their pastor's experience. The churches will almost certainly gain more than they give.

Chapter 6

For Witness In The City
(The Church and Home Mission)

Edwin Orton

Edwin Orton is the Director of the Birmingham City Mission. He trained at the College and at the Missionary School of Medicine and God gave him a world vision for city missionary work. He and his wife began church planting in 1953 and he founded the City Mission in 1966 while planting and pastoring the Kingshurst Evangelical Church. He is deeply involved in the whole City Mission scene both nationally and worldwide, and his initiative has led to the formation of several other city missions in Britain, Spain and India. He has travelled widely as Bible teacher, evangelist and pastor to missionaries and has a special interest in India. He is the author of *Into the City: the Challenge of Urban Mission.*

Chapter 6

For Witness In The City
(The Church and Home Mission)

Edwin Orton

My purpose in becoming a student at the Glasgow Bible
Training Institute in 1950 was to train for overseas mission.
There was no lack in this department. Each morning a
different continent had its own prayer meeting, and the
missionary meetings of the College provided a surfeit of
information and challenge. But the practical training was in
the city. Open air meetings, visitation in the tenements,
services in Barlinnie Prison, outreach to the lodging houses,
were all part of the regular training of the BTI. It was home
mission first, foreign missions next.

This was the pattern set by our Lord Jesus in his last words
to his disciples, 'You will be my witnesses in Jerusalem, and
in all Judea and Samaria, and to the ends of the earth' (Acts
1:8). In other words, start witnessing where you are, begin at
home and then keep on reaching out.

There is no doubt that most of our great missionaries had
their early training in some sort of home mission. It is equally
true that these missions have played a vital role in modern
church history and are an essential means of evangelising the
nations and giving practical expressions of the power of the
gospel.

Glasgow has the honour of being the birthplace of the
modern City Mission movement. David Nasmith founded the
first City Mission in 1826, probably the first interdenomina-

tional missionary society. His object was to 'extend the knowledge of the gospel among the inhabitants and its vicinity (especially the poor) without any reference to denominational distinction or peculiarity of Church Government'. Nasmith was a man of vision, faith and purpose with a fervent passion for souls. He founded missions throughout Britain, Ireland, America and France. Many of his missions, including the great London City Mission, still thrive today.

It is evident that there is greater need today for home missions, especially in the cities, than at any other time. The population has grown enormously, social evils abound and new generations are unreached by the gospel. It is true that in Britain and Western countries there is not the kind of poverty which existed in the 19th century, but there are many new needs among the people. Glue sniffing among the young is common, drug addiction is on the increase, prostitution, child abuse and sexually transmitted diseases are causing much human suffering. Largely because of family breakdown, homelessness is on the increase. The elderly are often neglected and subjected to violence. Crime has reached an all-time high level. The mass media caricature the gospel and the people continue to die in their sins and without hope.

The Nature of Home Mission

It is often said that if the church were doing its job there would be no need for para-church movements. That is to mistake the nature of a home mission. Such a society does not compete with the church and indeed does not stand apart from it. Work within the mission is no substitute for local church life and mission workers are expected to attend church for worship and live by its standards. On the other hand local churches are not necessarily equipped to meet needs which the missions they support are able to meet.

The work of the missions is to reach the unreached for Christ. Geographically there are many gaps between churches, but socially and vocationally there are more.

In the case of inner city churches there are special problems. One is, as Wesley put it, that he couldn't help it if the new converts became richer. They tend to be more provident, less watchful, of greater integrity, more industrious and, therefore, can be less liable to be unemployed. It is natural for them to want better housing for their families and better education for their children, therefore, they tend to move to the more affluent suburbs. If they are loyal to their inner city church they will continue to attend it, but will become strangers to that community.

As their children grow up they put down their own roots. The inner city church, therefore, lacks young people and the ageing church has less interest in outreach. Moreover, as the people leave the inner city their place is often taken either by new citizens from other lands, cultures and religions, or by the less able nationals who are often unresponsive to the gospel or in need of continued support.

The remedy is for people to respond to the challenge and move back to the city. This may mean making sacrifices, but they are nothing compared with those which overseas missionaries often have to make. But it also requires the employment of specialist missionaries who may need to learn other languages and study other cultures.

New approaches are required to reach the established community of elderly and needy people. Luncheon clubs, mother and toddler groups, drop-in centres and training centres for the unemployed can easily be fitted into existing church buildings. Regular systematic visitation of the neighbourhood and the development of home Bible study groups is essential for Christian outreach.

For such work the mission may need special training. In one situation in Birmingham the missionary found it necessary to spend a year in Pakistan learning the Urdu language and culture so that he could more effectively communicate with the Pakistani people in Birmingham.

Worldwide today there are more than 600 organisations which may be called City Missions. Many of these are networked together. One of the largest of these networks is the International Union of Gospel Missions which links almost 300 Rescue Missions, mainly in North America. Another group is the European Association of Urban Missions which gathers a triennial conference of missions from Germany, Scandinavia and many other European countries.

Among city missions of note is the great Berlin City Mission (Berliner Stadtmission) founded in 1877. Its work of evangelism and caring for human need has continued unabated through two world wars, surviving the Nazi era and it did magnificent work in the post-war years until the Berlin Wall was erected in 1961. With the division of the city came the division of the mission. Both halves continued their excellent work, the West Berlin City Mission thriving though surrounded by the wall, the East Berlin Mission ministering faithfully in spite of the restrictions of atheistic communism. Now that Germany is reunited, the Berlin City Mission is accepting the challenge of the new situation by reaching out to all sections of the community by wise declaration of the gospel and compassionate caring for the needy.

One of the largest home missions is the Sydney City Mission in Australia. A staff of several hundred committed Christians provides a variety of services from rehabilitation of young drug addicts to special care for the elderly and disabled. Their 'Startover' telephone counselling service is widely advertised and greatly used, being backed up by a fleet

of 'Missionbeat' rescue ambulances. The mission has gained
the respect of the Government for its work amongst the
homeless and unemployed. This Christian social work provides a platform for continuous personal evangelism as well
as a practical demonstration of the love of God in the city.

The scale and standard of the work of Australian City
Missions can be estimated in that Sydney City Mission has an
annual budget of more than £12,000,000. In Melbourne the
Mission has a hospice for terminally ill patients and also
industrial premises providing employment for rehabilitated
alcoholics and others. A number of new city missions have
opened in recent years in Australia.

The most southerly city missions are in Tasmania, with the
Launceston City Mission using a double-decker bus in its
outreach, and Hobart City Mission, founded by a London City
Missionary, still continuing as the oldest city mission in the
southern hemisphere.

In Europe, the Madrid City Mission began in the early
eighties. The changed political situation in Spain after the
death of Franco made new missionary work possible. Most of
this work is being done by foreign missionaries. In the case of
a city mission, however, the work is a home mission and,
therefore, is conducted by national workers within their own
culture.

Madrid City Mission is entirely Spanish. Two of its early
workers were trained in Birmingham City Mission; and the
writer has visited and encouraged the founding and growth of
the work. In less than ten years the Mission has developed a
programme of open-air evangelism and social care with
excellent premises in the city centre. Hundreds of people have
been helped by counselling, the provision of food and clothing along with the message of the gospel. A few full-time
workers are supported by a good number of voluntary work-

ers from churches of different denominations in the city. Financial support is also mainly raised locally.

In India the present Bombay City Mission is working mainly among Tamil people and led by Tamil workers. Formerly called the Bombay Prayer and Revival Band, the work was founded in 1979 and is developing rapidly into an effective home mission. It is an indigenous organisation conducted within the Indian culture by a dedicated group of about thirty full-time workers. Its headquarters is on the second floor of a rather poor apartment block. It has one vehicle, a small minibus donated by TEAR Fund, but its work is city-wide. Gospel preaching in the open air is done regularly. Several mission halls have been opened in the slums where some mission workers have moved to live among the people.

Specialist workers of the Bombay City Mission engage in rescue work among orphan children, lepers, prostitutes and addicts. Nursery schools provide care and basic Christian education for children of the very poor. Simple medicines are provided in a small clinic in one slum where 3,000,000 people live.

This account of the Bombay City Mission may cause some people to ask if such a work is not a home mission but a foreign mission. What is the difference between the two?

This question requires a careful examination of the special nature of home missions. Generally a foreign mission is a work conducted and supported by benefactors from overseas. A home mission is staffed and financed by individuals and churches in the land in which it operates. Such missions in the developing world may receive help from other countries but, as is the case of the Bombay City Mission, the administration and registration are local and the staff are home nationals.

If the home missions are in countries in which Christians

are in a minority, overseas support for such work is clearly a wise investment. The staff already know the local language and culture, can cope with the climate and conditions and need little training to communicate with their fellow countrymen. Nor do they require heavy travel expenses to get there or extensive time-out for furloughs in a far country. Involvement from abroad can be limited to financing certain capital projects, short-term training, encouragement visits and general prayer support.

Local churches support their home mission because it is their own mission. They can see what is being done and often benefit from the results. The mission provides a training ground for their own young people and an outlet for their desire to reach the whole of their cities and neighbourhoods with the gospel. Also, local leaders can be trustees, board members or committee members of the mission while the rest of their congregations can be involved as voluntary workers or prayer partners.

The Work of Home Missions

The briefest enquiry into the history of home missions in Britain will reveal a wealth of information regarding the effectiveness of their work in the past. This particularly applies to the Victorian period when the growth of towns and cities was at an unprecedented rate. Poverty was great and with it all the attendant evils. Evangelical Christians tackled the problems with great enthusiasm and hard endeavours. During this period the Salvation Army and Church Army were founded. The city and town missions joined many other societies in caring for the sick, elderly, destitute and disabled. Social needs of all kinds were addressed, but also the poor had the gospel preached to them.

During the twentieth century there has been a decline in the direct involvement of home mission with many social needs of the people. Perhaps this is due to the improved wealth and well-being of the nation, but it is also in line with the decline in church attendance. Yet much good is still being done by the great societies. In many cases the Government has recognised the value of such work and given financial support. This has often led to a scaling down of evangelistic activity or even a loss of church identity.

Today new challenges confront the Christian church and new initiatives are required. Although the old Gin Houses are a thing of the past, alcoholism in a more respectable guise is still a scourge to many families. Drug addiction, glue sniffing and the like are a serious problem for the young. The HIV virus and AIDS are an increasing threat with promiscuity and prostitution on the increase.

Above all, the spiritual needs of the people are compounded as the church and the gospel are grossly caricatured by the powerful media of the radio, television and press.

In dealing with the present situation and looking forward into the 21st century, home missions, and especially city missions, have exciting opportunities, using their vast experience and the principles which have applied successfully in the past.

First of all, a compassionate, personal contact must be made with individual people. Today's mass media lacks that human touch, and there is no alternative to one-to-one involvement in meeting human need. Children who are provided with expensive toys, television videos and computers, but are not shown personal love, are disturbed and insecure. Old people, even when supplied with adequate food and shelter, desperately need other people to visit and care for them. Dwellers in large, modern cities, especially those who live in apartments or flats, live isolated lives which cry out for personal friendship. Fear of violence and robbery adds to their loneliness.

There is a need for mission workers to visit local districts systematically and regularly, gently making known the love of God in Jesus Christ, and following up such visits with practical care appropriate to the situation. When this is carried out over a period of many months, the missionary becomes well known, accepted and trusted. A teaching ministry can take place by one-to-one Bible study or the development of house groups.

Caring work can be engaged in simultaneously with the verbal spread of the gospel. The link with the home opens the way to care for the whole family. One-parent families, which are on the increase, appreciate the offer of outings with a baby-sitting service. Unemployed people can be directed to training schemes and voluntary occupational activities. The elderly appreciate odd jobs being done in their homes or gardens. Lunch clubs, which provide opportunities to make new friendships, are welcome. Young mothers with toddlers, especially flat dwellers, can be helped by forming clubs for them.

Secondly, the city mission can be effective in dealing with people in the city who have special needs in the city. In Britain there is a move away from state provision, and many social services and voluntary organisations are being encouraged and assisted to fill the gap. Recently there has been a growth in homelessness. This is due not only to economic reasons, but also to family break-up and all kinds of social ills. Local churches feel incapable of dealing with these problems, but together they can support missions which have the structure and expertise to make provision of hostels and sheltered housing.

When people have been desperate for help, they have often

turned to the church. The resources of local churches to meet social needs are limited. It is also difficult for ministers to deal with people requiring professional attention, such as alcoholics and drug addicts. Here, trained home missionaries who deal with such problems daily can give real support to both clients and ministers. Local ministers can, therefore, refer clients to the mission just as a local doctor refers patients to a hospital. The mission itself may not be able to deal with all the referrals but has the means of networking with other agencies with specialist skills.

Regarding the meeting of practical needs, the mission is also of great importance. What minister has not been approached for money, food or shelter by some apparently destitute person? It is hard to distinguish the genuine from the fake. Referring such people to the mission is both practical and sensible; practical because it is impossible for local churches to carry stocks of food and clothing, or provide shelter, while the missions can; sensible because the minister can get on with his ministry without becoming too involved with time-consuming social problems, and the experienced missionaries can detect the real needs and deal with them.

The Value of Home Missions

The difference between church and mission must be clearly understood. The church by its nature is a community of those called out from the world to worship and serve God together. The missionaries are those who have been sent out by the church to reach the unreached for Christ. As we have seen, the two are not rivals but parts of a whole.

There are, of course, grey areas in which the church itself is involved in missions and where missionaries minister within the church.

For example, a church may hold its children's holiday

club, which may be an annual event lasting a week. The missionary, however, will seek to be reaching children in schools on a daily basis. He is able to do this because of his training and also because he is set free from secular work and can be in school during the working day. Church members run their clubs in their spare time.

The missionary's business is to declare the gospel in the market place, factory, college, hospital and prison. But he is no amateur in danger of bringing discredit to the gospel. His training and experience will inspire the confidence of the authorities to allow him to do his work unhindered. His work is usually quiet and personal, caring for the whole man. Often he is seen as a kind of welfare officer, visiting the sick, comforting the bereaved and counselling the anxious. But always he has the spiritual dimension, bringing Christ to the people just where they are.

There are still many people who, even if they wished to attend church, would find it difficult because of their working hours. Here the missionary has a social role. Many missions have workers who visit policemen or railway workers, busmen, cab drivers, firemen, hoteliers and others not free on Sundays. In some cases security vetting is required, or even specialised professional training.

The home missionary is no transient. He is not involved in a brief crusade which may be soon forgotten. He aims to be as well known as the community policeman on his beat or the local doctor, and at least as reliable as they are. His patch is geographical, regardless of denominational or social boundaries. To all the churches in the district he is known as 'our missionary'. Sometimes he speaks on their behalf representing them before the bureaucrats and politicians. Often he is the only contact which officialdom has with the church. Through him the church is represented for what it does rather than what it says.

Such home missions make ideal training ground for ministers and foreign missionaries. Understanding human nature is not developed in the classroom. Sin and its results are not theories but realities when seen where people live. Salvation is a glorious truth when it is seen to work at street level. Many pastors and Christian workers had their practical training in the city missions. Some were brought to Christ there.

In recent years a number of missions have developed short courses for young people which have been both informative and character building. The courses enhance spirituality and give theology concrete expression. The experience is testing but stimulating, sometimes serving as a crucial interlude between college and career. At the same time the students do a valuable job, enjoy community life and learn to communicate.

The Founding of Home Missions

When Abraham set out for the promised land, he did not know where he was going. He went in the obedience of faith, thus illustrating the chief principles of founding a work for God. It must come as a result of his will and calling. Nevertheless it may be helpful here to record in outline our own experience in founding city missions.

The Birmingham City Mission came into being as a result of a burden which would not go away but grew greater over several years. At least two people in different cities had prayed for the formation of a mission in Birmingham for thirty years. When the first meeting was held, fifteen people were present from eight different churches of various denominations. Both business meetings and prayer meetings were held monthly. Four months after the first meeting, outreach began in the form of visitation on a new housing estate and open air preaching in the city centre. Within six months a weekend conference was held in the country, attended by about thirty participants who were addressed by a senior member of another established mission.

In the early stages finance and property were not high on the list of priorities. The recruiting of prayer partners was. Committee members were themselves compassionate activists experienced in Christian service. They led from the front in evangelism and care for the needy.

Discussion took place regarding Christian doctrine and agreement was gained on basic truths which were clearly biblical and held in common by most denominations. Methods were considered but left open, allowing for different traditions and abilities and with the changes of a modern world in mind.

The first expenditure incurred was the purchase of means of communication; typewriter, duplicator and public address equipment. A small property in the city centre was rented cheaply and furnished at little cost. That served as office, enquiry room, evangelistic base, store and chapel. Enthusiastic volunteers prepared the building and became involved in the outreach.

It was more than three years before a paid full-time worker was engaged, and then only temporarily. In those early days the mission achieved much by mobilising churches for special events, convening evangelistic meetings and sponsoring training courses.

By this time a Trust Deed was completed by a solicitor and the mission registered with the Charity Commission. A chairman, secretary and treasurer were appointed, minutes kept of all committee meetings and accounts kept and audited.

BCM was formally inaugurated in October 1966 at a meeting attended by more than 200 people from 50 different churches of several denominations. A monthly newsletter was circulated and some years later a quarterly magazine and annual report were published.

The finding of suitable missionaries was a problem to us for some years. We needed experienced workers but they were not available. Possibly it was because we were a mission with little finance and poor publicity. However, some of those who worked voluntarily were willing to shorten their working week and work part-time for the mission on low pay. Young people began to apply for short-term service and some asked to join the staff.

From the beginning we were encouraged by the results. Here and there people experienced conversion and told us their stories. This spurred us on to greater efforts and our enthusiasm was high. We also received many wonderful answers to prayer in the provision of money, goods, property and people.

It was not that we planned the work carefully. One thing simply led to another, though each step was covered in prayer.

At first we found that wherever we held open-air meetings in the city we would be accosted by people asking for money - 'the price of a cup of tea'. We responded by giving small amounts but we soon discovered that it was not always tea they wanted to drink. When the evangelistic centre was opened we took them there and gave them food and drink rather than money. Some people were obviously in desperate need of clothing. This was soon supplied by our supporters but led to us developing a warehouse. Because of the problems of clients arriving in penny numbers at odd times we arranged opening hours when they could congregate and not only receive physical care but have the gospel preached to them.

Working closely with homeless people gave us an insight into their culture and needs. Many were sleeping in the crypt of the Roman Catholic Cathedral when in 1978 there was a fire and all were turned out into the winter snow. We could do no other than open our centre as an emergency shelter. This resulted in BCM praying for more suitable accommodation and in 1979 prayers were answered and the Mission acquired a hostel for homeless people in the city centre.

Space does not allow us to give details here, but the reader can imagine the efforts required in engaging staff, organising day and night cover, dealing with difficult clients, providing food, laundry and keeping the place warm and clean.

God makes no mistakes. He leads if we will follow. He provides if we will trust him. We have found repeatedly that when he has called us into some new venture he has already prepared workers to do the job. Usually we had to move forward without sufficient funds but we have always found that they have not been far behind. We must act in faith but he always responds to our trust.

The Future of Home Missions

Half of the world's population now lives in cities. In the 1980s one billion people moved from rural to urban areas. Another billion will move in the 1990s. These movements create enormous problems, but they also present great opportunities.

World cities are growing at an ever-increasing rate. Mexico City, with its population of twenty-three millions, is growing at the rate of one million each year. Two million homeless children live on its streets. In the three largest cities of the world, forty-five per cent live in appalling slums. Most people throughout the world face an urban future.

Changes in Eastern Europe have revealed the state of cities in which the population has grown amid atheism and uneconomic industrialism. The clamour for material relief is matched only by a thirst for spiritual regeneration.

Economic recession in the West has left its cities with declining industry and increasing unemployment. The unprecedented crime rate and community unrest are symptomatic of the disillusionment, frustration and spiritual impoverishment of today's city dwellers. People move to the city looking for work and a better lifestyle. They find that the progress of technology and automation has led to fewer jobs, especially for semi-skilled or unskilled labourers. Factories stand empty. Less money leads to poorer housing, urban decay and low morale.

Children brought up in such conditions face a bleak future. Many are unable to find work on leaving school. Some are in the second or even third generation of unemployment. The frustration is exacerbated by television advertising and displays in shop windows of goods which they will never be able to afford. Some turn to shoplifting and housebreaking while others hide from reality in glue sniffing or drug taking.

Meeting the social needs of the poor seems to the state like pouring wealth into a bottomless pit. The more that is provided, the more that is needed. Government has, therefore, tended to tighten controls and make access to relief more difficult. The uneducated and inadequate suffer more.

All these developments in urban life provide a wide field for the cultivation of home missions. Never before have they been needed so much. David Nasmith, William Booth, Dr Barnardo, Lord Shaftesbury and others would have leapt to the challenge which is so much greater than in their day.

Every city is a mission field. Some contain large overseas communities of people we could hardly have read about a generation ago. Many languages are spoken and religions followed.

There is a vast ignorance of the Christian message. Most citizens do not attend church, send children to Sunday School, read the Bible or know its teaching. To most people the church is an alien culture, an aberration, an irrelevance.

Home missions, especially city missions, must now address themselves to new and positive actions. The authorities would often welcome the practical involvement of such voluntary societies and even grant financial support. But such help must be regarded as supplementary only.

The need is for missionaries who will become activists. Each city has its own special needs and each mission will have its own emphasis. The starting point must always be that of Moses. God said to him, 'What is that in your hand?' Too often Christian people wait for someone else to take the initiative, someone with better gifts, more training, longer experience. But all things are possible to him who believes.

There will be no lack of clients; they are crying out for help of every kind. That the need is not all physical can be clearly seen in the vast industry in horoscopes and the occult. The resurgence of Islam, Buddhism, Hinduism and other religions and cults shouts out the human need for God. A positive and compassionate declaration of the Christian gospel will not fall on deaf ears when it is accompanied by good works. Jesus went about doing good and, whatever the opposition, so must we.

A modern city mission is ideally placed to demonstrate the love of God in word and deed to a large number of people. To be successful it must, in function and method, be relevant to the people's needs. It should be seen to be modern, efficient and well managed. A consistent Christian testimony and a reputation for reliable service must be nurtured. Funds need to be used economically but in a progressive and professional manner. Financial integrity is essential.

The spiritual tone of the home mission needs to be constantly maintained, with a sense of the presence of God. Prayer, Bible teaching and worship should be natural ingredients of the daily life of the mission, and prayer meetings part of the normal routine. The beliefs of the society need to be clearly stated. They should not be so ambiguous as to be meaningless and not so doctrinaire as to exclude those who differ on non-essentials yet are genuine Christians.

In Britain, as elsewhere in the world, there is a need for new city missions, because new cities have arisen and also because some cities have never had such missions or, if they did, they no longer function. It is also true that some city missions are in need of rejuvenation and extension.

Opportunities abound on every hand. Schools often welcome mission workers. Their interdenominational stance and their caring ministry are particularly attractive. Elderly people learn to trust the local missionaries and welcome them into their homes and appreciate the services provided. The homeless, the destitute, the broken and rejected all appreciate the kindness and practical help given them by the mission. From such hopeless situations many have been rescued in the past and many await the helping hand.

The future of city missions is exciting and challenging. This is the time to rise and build. The ancient call made to Jonah is still with us, 'Go to the great city and preach against it, because its wickedness has come up before me.' To those who would respond the Lord says, as he did to Paul on the Damascus Road, 'Now get up and go into the city, and you will be told what you must do.'

Chapter 7

And In All The World
(The Church and World Mission)

Stanley Davies and David Ellis

Rev Stanley Davies is the General Secretary of the Evangelical Missionary Alliance. He trained as a cartographical draughtsman and surveyor and worked in many countries of Africa and Asia. After missionary training at the College, he commenced service in East Africa with the Africa Inland Mission in 1965 and was involved in many different forms of missionary activity, including youth work, theological training and mission administration. In 1980 he was appointed Director of Mission Studies at Moorlands Bible College, where he served until he began his present work with the EMA in 1983. He has considerable Council involvement with a number of missionary societies and other evangelical organisations.

Rev David Ellis has been British Home Director of the Overseas Missionary Fellowship since 1989. He trained as an engineer before becoming a student at the College. He married the Principal's daughter and under the OMF they worked with the church in Java for over 20 years, concentrating on church planting, evangelism and lay training. He became the mission's Indonesian Area Director and then, in Singapore, its Director of Overseas Ministries. In 1983 he began work as a Church of Scotland minister at St George's Tron Church, Glasgow as Associate to the Rev Eric Alexander. He has written various Christian books in the Indonesian language and writes a regular column in East Asia Millions.

Chapter 7

And In All The World
(The Church and World Mission)

Stanley Davies and David Ellis

'In the beginning God' - we need to look no further to find the ground of mission. We do not argue from the state of the world to God but from God to the state of the world.

In Christ we know we have found the one who can meet the needs of a fallen world. But we do not embark on mission first and foremost because we believe that. Our starting-point must be that we embark on mission because we believe God, the Saviour of the world, wills to save this fallen world and he sent his Son Jesus to do just that. The initiative and the ground of mission are his. This cardinal principle must undergird mission if it is not to lose its way in the next century.

The pressure is to accommodate our rationale for mission to the man-centred, problem-oriented thought patterns that govern the age. Seeing people and their physical deprivations and suffering as motivation for mission has become more acceptable. To place the emphasis on the central truth that 'God was reconciling the world to himself in Christ ... and has committed to us the ministry of reconciliation' (2 Corinthians 5:19) has become less popular. It is more fashionable to be tackling the symptoms of humanity's alienation from God rather than its cause. It is fashionable to want to exorcise the demons of Racism, Apartheid, Sexism, Colonialism, Capitalism or Communism and shift the centre of mission from God, the absolute, self-existent Creator to man, the finite dependent creature.

Twentieth-century man has a blinkered, subjective perspective. His social and personal needs have increasingly taken centre stage. There is little or no acknowledgment of the need for redemption and reconciliation. The centre pivot of mission has become man not God. 'God', thus marginalised becomes whatever you wish to choose him to be - a far more comfortable concept in today's multi-faith society. Yet a God totally impotent to deal with the root of man's problem - his alienation.

To say that is not to dismiss the need for mission to tackle the symptoms of our alienation from God. The gospel is for the whole person or it is no gospel. It speaks to man's inhumanity to man. It reaches out to the hungry. It is good news to the poor. It cares for the widows and the fatherless. But if it is not to lose its way, it is imperative that it starts with the presupposition, 'in the beginning God'.

Get that wrong and everything else goes wrong. Someone has pointed out that before Galileo the earth was thought to be the centre of our planetary system and scientists had endless problems. It was only when it was discovered that the sun was central that everything else fell into place. In the same way it will only be if the church recognises God to be both the starting-point and centre of mission that it will be true to its calling to mission.

The fundamental nature of mission derives from the character of God. It is what we believe about him that determines what we believe about mission. He is the unique self-existent 'I am', the one who appeared to Moses in the flame of fire that did not depend for its existence on the combustible material of the bush. He is the one who exists, the one who needs nothing to be, the one who made everything, the one who flung the stars into space and lavished infinite care on the smallest atom. As the Psalmist reminds us again and again, the whole universe is a declaration of his being, his wisdom, love and power.

Humanity, created in 'God's own image' as the crown of his creation, shows us a whole new dimension of God's character. Placed as vicegerent to have authority over the created order, man was tempted to doubt and disobey. It was then he discovered that just as there were physical laws in the universe so too the Creator had set moral laws. Jump off a cliff and the law of gravity decides your fate. Sin and you reap sin's wages. It is decreed by God's moral law.

Such laws were designed for man's safety and well-being, to preserve the liberty and freedom of the creature to operate within the design parameters of the Creator. As rails to the train, so God's moral laws were laid to preserve life. God wanted men and women to enjoy the paradise he had created for them. Tragically in their disobedience they discovered that their sin exposed them inevitably to the judgment of God.

Yet in the darkness of their guilt people hear the voice of God calling out to them as he did to Adam in the Garden of Eden, 'Where are you?' It is the voice of one who 'so loved the world that he sent his only Son' into it to be its Saviour. For while the wrath of God burns to consume all unholiness it does not burn with vindictiveness but with an extraordinary, righteous and saving love. The only picture we have in Scripture of God in a hurry is when he, as the father, runs to embrace the penitent prodigal. God takes 'no pleasure in the death of the wicked' (Ezekiel 18:32) and indeed is 'not willing that any should perish but that all should come to repentance' (2 Peter 3:9).

'God prefers salvation to judgment. Herein lies the missionary element. God's wrath makes the gospel necessary. His love makes it possible' (Kane). His righteous saving love reaches out to save by making men and women righteous. He knows that to bring men and women into fellowship with himself, to bring them to the 'obedience of faith', to have them living voluntarily under his rule and lordship is to have them fulfilling their design-potential. God's holiness is not passive and simply judgmental and damning but active, recreative and saving. That is the gospel.

Now for men and women to fulfil their design-potential is to bring glory to their Creator. That is our concern - to bring glory to God. That is why we pray, 'Your kingdom come'. That is why we go to make disciples of all nations. For it is over all nations God rules. 'The LORD has established his throne in the heaven and his kingdom rules over all' (Psalm 103:19). 'For God is the King of all the earth ... God reigns over the nations ... the kings of the earth belong to God ...' (Psalm 47:7-9).

The early chapters of Genesis show us the morass into which one man's sin brought the whole of creation. Out of that morass God chose one man, Abraham, and brought him to the obedience of faith that, through that man, he might establish a nation where his kingship would be acknowledged. His election of that nation Israel was for the blessing of the whole world. They were to be a holy nation, separate and distinct from the nations. They were to be God's servant 'in whom I will display my splendour ...' (Isaiah 49:3), and they were chosen to become '... a light for the Gentiles that you may bring my salvation to the ends of the earth ...' (Isaiah 49:6).

In all of that Israel failed miserably. They chose a human monarchy rather than accept theocracy, yet graciously in their pursuit of earthly kings God foreshadowed the day when the divine king would come and his rule would be established in their hearts. The coronation Psalm (Psalm 2) speaks prophetically of 'great David's greater son' when it says ' ''I have installed my King on Zion, my holy hill ... '' ''You are my Son; today I have become your Father. Ask of me, and I will make the nations your inheritance, the ends of the earth your possession. You will rule them ... '' ' The nations of the earth are his rightful inheritance. They are his by right of creation. They are his by right of divine election. They are his by right of redemption. This is what Paul underlines when he says, 'therefore God exalted him to the highest place and gave him the name that is above every name, that at the name of Jesus every knee should bow ... ' (Philippians 2:9-10).

And it is to that ultimate picture that all Scripture points as we see the veil removed at the end of time and we find John saying, 'After this I looked and there before me was a great multitude that no one could count, from every nation, tribe, people and language, standing before the throne and in front of the Lamb ... And they cried out in a loud voice, ''Salvation belongs to our God who sits on the throne and to the Lamb''' (Revelation 7: 9-10).

So the kingdoms of this world are to become the kingdoms of our God and of his Christ and the earth is to be 'filled with the knowledge of the LORD as the waters cover the sea' (Isaiah 11:9) for Christ is established as 'the Saviour of the world' (I John 4:14) - not 'a saviour' nor 'one of the saviours' but 'the Saviour'.

It was with the full consciousness of the promises of Psalm 2 and the ultimate fulfilment of Revelation 7 that Jesus stood before his disciples and could say, 'All authority in heaven and on earth have been given to me. *Therefore* go and make disciples of all nations ...'

The royal command only has one legitimate response - obedience. And the paramount reason why we are to be involved in mission to all nations is because it is writ large in the heart of our Creator-God and nothing in our 20th century world can ever change that. The initiative for mission is in the character of our unchanging God.

Just as the people of God were called under the old covenant to be a 'light for the nations ... that you may bring my salvation to the ends of the earth ...' so Jesus called out his people (Matthew 16:18), through the new covenant in his blood, to be light and salt, light to bring spiritual and moral clarity, salt to be a preserving influence in a corrupt society.

As those who have been reconciled to God through his Son dying our death, we know what it is to be freed of all charges against us, so that we are compelled by the realisation of that love shown to us to plead with all men everywhere that they be reconciled to God. The obligation is on us to preach (I Corinthians 9:16) for we are debtors to all men since entering into the blessings of the gospel. Incredibly from being debtors we have been exalted to the rank of being ambassadors. We have the highest honour as his ambassadors and witnesses (Acts 1:8) to engage in mission.

We engage in mission, not because we want to, but because we are under divine rule and command. We see it as the highest privilege. Knowing that our risen Lord and God has placed us under his command to go and preach and make disciples, we need no further mandate!

Our Master was sent to do the will of his Father; to pour out his life; to serve and not to be served; to make himself of no reputation; to take the form of a servant; to live with no place to rest his head; to accept suffering and death, even death on a cross. As he showed his disciples the evidence of his obedience in his nail-scarred hands, he said, 'As the Father has sent me, I am sending you' (John 20:21).

Nothing about this world-commission has changed. Nothing in the character of our God, who is the ground of mission, could change. But there is something that has to change and change rapidly if the church is not to lose the place as it looks at world mission in the 21st century. Somehow we have to come to terms with the need for a fundamental shift in our perception of the world in which we live as it affects mission- ary outreach.

Wander through the marble tombs of St Paul's in London and you cannot help being aware of imperial history and of the nineteenth-century perspective on the world. Thinking went more or less in a straight line. Britain was here and the rest of the world was somewhere over there. If you were not British you were 'foreign'. Missions growing as they did in that soil inevitably found some of the imperialistic mud sticking to their boots.

Our comfortable insular parochialism would, of course, still like to have the luxury of being able to put a cocoon around its thinking. It is easier to think of missions and cross- cultural issues as being somehow 'out there'. But take a second look at those milling around the tombs in St Paul's and all around you see men and women of every 'nation, tribe, people and language ...' staring uncomprehendingly at the relics of British jingoism as they click their Nikon auto-focus cameras. The demographic map has changed. Modern tech- nology has revolutionised the globe. 'They' are no longer 'over there'. 'They' are right here where we live.

World mission has moved from being a simple straight- line distinction of *home* and *abroad*, to the second of which a few dedicated souls are called to commit themselves. It is more a question of concentric circles, not straight lines, that ought to shape our thinking. Not that the mission has really changed. What has to change is an over-simplistic perception of it.

We are called to be light. Light shines in a 360⁰ degree circle. It shines in the immediate vicinity. It shines in ever-increasing circles, starting at the point of origin.

That more biblical perception needs to reshape the church's practical involvement in mission. The major issue of world mission is not one of geography. The major issue of world mission is 'who is my neighbour?' And we may find the answer today just as uncomfortable as those Jews Jesus shocked with his story of 'the good Samaritan'. The call to each of us is to become a 'world Christian' right where we are.

Of course, there are still many millions of unreached peoples 'out there'. Our calling to go to them is unchanged. But unreached peoples can no longer be seen as being only those who are 'far, far away in heathen darkness dwelling'. Many of them are right 'here on the street where you live'. That challenges the integrity of our professed vision for mission. If we pray ardently for the conversion of Arab nations or that God will 'bless the dear people of Pakistan' how do our prayers stand up when we meet them at that corner shop which is always there when we need an extra pound of sugar? Demographic changes have taken place all around us. They challenge our comfortable evangelical traditions about world mission. World mission has come to our doorstep. How open are our doors? How much are we 'world Christians' when it comes to the local realities of Bradford or Glasgow?

On the world scene the immense changes that have taken place in recent years throughout the former communist countries of Eastern Europe and the old Soviet Union (now the Commonwealth of Independent States) have provided new challenges for the churches of Western Europe. Many congregations in Western Europe have become involved with aid and compassionate action in countries like Romania and Albania. This has sometimes been without consultation or any attempt to co-ordinate their efforts with specialist agencies that have vast experience of those countries. The results have often led to duplication, insensitive paternalism or even counter-productive efforts that hinder rather than help the development of the churches in those countries.

On the other hand, the incredible new opportunities for Christian professionals to assist these countries with all kinds of skills and experience is often unknown or ignored. We need a new generation of entrepreneurs and risk-takers, professionally competent and cross-culturally trained to enter these countries and witness for Christ in a wide range of exciting openings. The old category of 'tentmakers' is still a valid way of entering countries. Different groups use different titles for this category of worker. However, churches throughout Europe should be equipping their members to move out across the world with the clear aim of making Christ known to those with whom they work, and seeking to disciple those who confess Christ in their communities.

Another major factor in world mission is the shift in demographic terms between the rural and urban populations of the world. This must have a major bearing on mission strategy in the coming decades. Throughout the history of the human race the migration of people from one area to another has provided the background to changes in population. These migrations have largely been of rural populations who sometimes moved peacefully to another area, while on other occasions such movements had violent consequences, leading to conflict and domination of one group by another.

Today's immigration pattern is towards the cities of the south and east. 'Vast slums and shanty towns have developed that present tremendous problems for urban planners who work on severely limited budgets' (T. Monsma). While urban centres in India and China go back to ancient times, the growth that has taken place recently in both those countries is now reaching crisis levels. Tremendous growth has also taken place in Africa and Latin America. David Barratt has estimated that by the year 2020 there will be nine major cities of the world with a population greater than 20 million inhabitants, cities like Mexico City (35), Shanghai (35), Beijing (30), Sao Paulo (28), Bombay (25), Calcutta (24), Jakarta (22) and Tokyo/Yokohama (21).

Here is an immense challenge to the global missionary movement. Cities need targeting as prime areas in which to launch new mission projects. This will mean mobilising new kinds of teams compared to those recruited in previous generations.

Yet another inescapable dynamic in the changing face of world missions is the discernible shift in the political and economic balance of power from West to East. If the 19th century marked the rise of the British Empire and the present century that of the United States, the next century may be that of the Asian Pacific nations. The economic resurgence of the fire-breathing industrial dragons along the Western Pacific rim is giving them power and economic muscle. Japan, Korea, Taiwan and China are all moving rapidly to exert more and more influence. While it is true that the greatest number of unreached people still live in East Asia, where less than five per cent know Christ, the revolutionary pace of life and the dynamic changes taking place in these nations are affecting the whole church in Asia.

As it looks at the year 2,000 the Korean Church is praying and planning to send 10,000 missionaries. Given the dynamic of its peoples and the sovereign purposes of our God, we may yet find we are about to witness a new missionary movement such as has not been seen this century.

If that does happen then the traditional pattern of our British understanding of world missions will inevitably have to change yet again. The mould in which our thinking has rested for more than a hundred years will have to go. The distinction between 'here and there' that has characterised our thinking is outdated. World missions are not the optional luxury of a few super-saints. Rather we are all called to be 'world Christians' here! We face the reality today where our 'ends of the earth' are some other Christian's 'Jerusalem'.

So around the world the Spirit of God is stirring the church to cross barriers and boundaries with the gospel. A new era has dawned in India where very few western missionaries are permitted to enter. Today, however, there are thousands of Indian cross-cultural missionaries moving throughout the sub-continent planting churches cross-culturally in areas where the church is weak or non-existent. Two hundred years after William Carey entered India the picture is very different from the one that confronted him on his arrival, but the challenge to the churches of India is still immense. The Indian Missions Association seeks to assist this dynamic movement with training, advice and by setting standards for newly emerging mission agencies. Resistance by militant Hindus has meant that progress has often only been accomplished at great cost.

In West Africa new missionary fervour is sweeping through the churches. One example is the Evangelical Missionary Society, associated with the Evangelical Churches of West Africa, which has sent out over eight hundred cross-cultural workers both within Nigeria as well as beyond its borders to other countries of West Africa. Many are seeking to witness to Muslim peoples in the Sahel region of Africa often at great cost to themselves and their families.

In Brazil in the last ten years new mission agencies have been formed that are now sending Brazilian missionaries into different areas of the world. Some are working in Muslim countries in pioneer situations. Others are working in various

Portuguese-speaking nations such as Angola and Mozambique. Throughout Latin America the COMIBAM movement is providing a valuable network for the emerging missionary movement from Argentina to Mexico.

Wherever we look today in the two-thirds world, we can identify a new missionary zeal. In the Pacific Islands, throughout Indonesia, the Philippines and many countries of sub-Sahara Africa, God is stirring his people to reach out beyond their own cultural and linguistic boundaries. Many of these witnesses are carrying on their work quietly, without publicity, unknown as far as the western church is concerned. They are, however, known to the Lord of the Harvest who has recorded their exploits in his book as he did those of the saints of old in Hebrews 11. He will honour their faith and sacrifice for the gospel.

Where does this leave the church in the west? What should be our response to such dynamic movements?

Some react with resignation, giving the impression that the west has done its part, for better or for worse, and therefore the task should be left to the churches of the south and east. Others bemoan the situation of church decline in Europe and say that the priority should be to engage in mission at home before attempting to take the gospel any further.

Surely neither of these options is correct. Yes, we desperately need help from the church in Africa and Asia and Latin America to re-evangelise our needy continent. We must learn how to ask for that help and how to welcome the contribution of African evangelists and Latin American church planters with their passion, love and simple life-style. At the same time the non-western missionary movements are calling for real partnership in solving some of the problems they are encountering in their missionary efforts.

Some of their problems are ones that the western mission-

ary movement has grappled with for decades or even centuries. There are problems like providing adequate cross-
cultural training, acquiring linguistic expertise, the pastoral
care of workers in remote areas, the need for adequate care of
missionary families and, in particular, the education of the
children of missionaries. Many of these are new obstacles to
the newly-formed mission agencies from Korea to Kenya but
they are old ones to the western agencies. There is a need for
sensitive sharing of experience and resources, so that together
we may learn from one another in a new era of global mission.

The Missions Commission of the World Evangelical Fellowship has been established to assist this process of exchange
and sharing of resources. By bringing together key leaders of
mission agencies from the west, the east and the south, it
provides a network to facilitate the interchange of information, the visits of consultants and the identification of specific
needs that require action for effective cross-cultural mission
anywhere in the world.

Other agencies such as the Lausanne Movement for World
Evangelisation and the AD 2000 Movement have concen-
trated on the evangelisation of specific countries and peoples
by the churches in those countries. Both have been instrumen-
tal in inspiring, informing and challenging individuals to
become involved in world evangelisation.

Some churches in the west that used to be involved in
sending missionary personnel seem to have become para-
lysed. This paralysis has been caused by a combination of
factors such as the following :

1. The acceptance of an incipient universalism that has
blunted the doctrines once held by their forefathers and
the willingness to accept other religions as being equally
valid ways to God as the Christian gospel.

2. A post-colonial hangover that bemoans the problems associated with the western missionary movement's close identification with the colonial era and the loss of confidence in sharing the gospel out of a sense of weakness instead of a position of strength.

3. The acceptance of a form of partnership with churches overseas that has come into being through their own missionary activities but that now limits them to participate in the affairs of those churches on restrictive terms. This has led some western churches to understand that their task has been virtually completed and they have, therefore, simply entered into fraternal relationships and provided exchange programmes for one another.

Each of these factors has blinded many western churches to the stark fact that there are still vast numbers in our world who have never heard the gospel of Christ, have no copy of the Scriptures in their language and no way of discovering the truth for themselves.

New forms of partnership between the western churches and those in the north, the east and the south must be discovered. Resources need to be pooled until every tribe, language group, nation and people have had an opportunity to understand the good news of Jesus Christ for themselves.

For over three centuries the burden of taking the gospel to the unreached peoples of the world has been largely carried by the west. Now younger churches all over the globe are stirring with vision to reach out. The great challenge is to creative partnership. As many missions open their ranks to members from all nations, so now the church in the west must broaden its thinking to find new dimensions of partnership.

When Paul describes Titus and Philemon as 'partners' he

uses a word derived from the word 'fellowship'. To his partner Philemon in verse 17 J B Phillips paraphrases Paul as saying, 'you and I have so much in common'. This is the attitude that must undergird our partnership. We have 'so much in common' with our sister churches. We share the same commission.

The commission has never been withdrawn from us. Mission is not something that can ever be delegated. The challenge remains unchanged.

Each local church in the west today ought to be vitally involved in praying, supporting, sending and working to take the gospel to at least one group of people that have yet to know Jesus Christ for themselves. It will require renewed vision and creative thinking as well as determined persistence until there is a viable church amongst that group, clan, tribe, people or nation. It should involve the whole church from the eldest to the youngest. It will involve the sharing of life as well as love, finance as well as people, suffering as well as joy.

There is a whole world to be won. The task will never be finished before Jesus comes again.

> Facing a task unfinished,
> That drives us to our knees,
> A task that, undiminished,
> Rebukes our slothful ease.
> We, who rejoice to know Thee,
> Renew before Thy throne
> The solemn pledge we owe Thee
> To go and make Thee known.

> (Bishop Frank Houghton)

Chapter 8

Both Today And Tomorrow
(The Church Statistically)

Peter Brierley

Peter Brierley has been European Director of World Vision/Marc Europe since 1983, training Christian leaders in a more effective use of their resources for evangelism and growth. He gained a London degree in Statistics before training at the College. For some years he did statistical work for the British government and he has done a vast amount of research for churches and missionary societies. He masterminded the UK Christian Handbook from its earliest beginnings and has so far done Christian Handbook research for nine European countries. He has council and committee links with many Christian organisations and is Research Associate for the Lausanne Committee for World Evangelisation.

Chapter 8

Both Today And Tomorrow
(The Church Statistically)

Peter Brierley

'We are what we have been becoming', someone once said. That is as true for organisations and churches as it is for individuals. It is just that the timescale may be different. The 20th century has not seen the decline and fall of religion as the Communists predicted 70 years ago, but instead the world has seen the challenge and growth of Christianity. The world, that is, except in the West where Christian fortunes have been rather different.

The implication of the quotation above is that we will be what we have become - unless by looking into the future we react now to ensure that some of the endemic trends are changed by positive action, prayerful attention and persuasive arguments. Apart from revival, Western Christianity is much like a modern cargo ship - well filled with important material, slow moving (in comparison to other forms of transport) and hard to change direction speedily. But Asian and South American Christianity is more akin to a pleasure liner on a cruise - full of enthusiasm and adventure, following a definite sense of purpose and able to take quick advantage of happenings en route. Both ships will sail for a long time yet. How can we who are on board the one learn from the other? By noting the trends, and determining to act.

People fall into three categories: they either make it happen, let it happen or, watch it happen. Which type are you?

It is possible to change your type if you are sufficiently motivated. Part of the motivation can come through assessing the implications of the direction in which the church is heading. Research is useful only so long as it leads to movement and change.

Nehemiah inspected the walls of Jerusalem, formed his strategy and then mobilised the populace. This chapter inspects the walls. The consequential strategy and mobilisation belong to the reader, but unless there is a willingness to act on the implications and get ready for the next millennium, then there is no point in inspecting the walls. What might we find as we inspect church walls at the end of the 20th century?

1. The Increasing Size and Influence of the Church

In his annual statistical table on Global Mission[1] David Barrett shows that not only are the number of Christians in the world increasing but their percentage is increasing also. In 1980 there were 1,400,000,000 Christians in the world, 32.8% of the world's 4,400,000,000 people. By 1991, the number had grown to 1,800,000,000 and the percentage to 33.3%. On present trends the number in the year 2000 is likely to be 2,100,000,000 and the percentage 34.1%. Between 1980 and 1991, on average 90,000 people were added to the churches each day, two-fifths just by being born into a church family. But between 1991 and 2000, we can expect 102,000 people to be added every day, only a third of whom will be children. In other words, David Barrett is predicting an increase in the rate of growth in the next decade, and an increase in the number of adults being reached as well.

These numbers vary by continent, as shown in Table 1. David Barrett defines a church member as any person who calls himself or herself a Christian, and will thus include many nominal Christians in his figures. The overall numbers of active Christians will, therefore, be less but the growth rates indicated are likely to be similar.

Table 1 : *Number of Church Members by Continent 1980-2000*

Continent	Church Members			Average percentage	
	1980 millions	1991 millions	2000E millions	1980/ 1991 %	1991/ 2000 %
Europe	420	430	440	+0.2	+0.3
Latin America	360	470	590	+2.5	+2.6
North America	190	200	210	+0.5	+0.5
Africa	170	250	340	+3.6	+3.5
South Asia	110	150	200	+2.9	+3.2
Old Soviet Union	100	110	120	+0.9	+1.0
East Asia	20	100	140	+15.8	+3.8
Oceania	20	20	20	0.0	0.0
Total Church members	1,390	1,730	2,060	+2.0	+2.0
World Population	4,370	5,380	6,250	+1.9	+1.7

Europe may have had the largest number of church members in 1980, but it was behind Latin America by 1991. The overall rate of growth per year between 1980 and 1991 is 2.0%, remarkably constant. Not everyone agrees with David Barrett's figures. Tom Houston, International Director of the Lausanne Committee on World Evangelisation, in a book *A Scenario Status of World Evangelisation 1991-2000* puts a higher growth in India (South Asia) and a much lower growth in Africa[2].

The huge jump between 1980 and 1991 in East Asia reflects the explosion of the House Church revival in the vast country of China in the 1980s. Africa's remarkably high growth in 1991-2000 is largely due to the continuing high population growth.

So the church is undoubtedly growing and, in terms of proportion, growing faster than the world population. It will, as a consequence grow in influence as well, but how far will that influence be real and how far imaginary? How do we prepare people to be more influential? Largely by urging them to act as true salt and clear light. Christians should not seek power for power's sake but influence in a humble fashion, after the pattern of Christ exemplified in Philippians 2. The church needs to teach its members more about being salt in society, acting with integrity, uprightness and honesty. The teaching it gives, therefore, is vital and its interface with society critical for the 1990s. We truly need to be guided as to how to be in the world but not of the world.

This church growth will particularly occur amongst the Pentecostals and Charismatics, as the figures in Table 2 make clear.

Table 2 : *Number of Pentecostals/Charismatics 1980-2000*

	Church members			Average percentage change per year	
	1980 millions	1991 millions	200E millions	1980/ 1991 %	1991/ 2000 %
Pentecostal/ Charismatic	150	380	540	+8.9	+4.0
Non Pentecostal /Charismatic	1,240	1,350	1,520	+0.8	+1.3
Total Church members	1,390	1,730	2,060	+2.0	+2.0
Percentage Pentecostal/ Charismatics of the total	11%	22%	26%		

Pentecostals/Charismatics moved from being 11% of the world's Christendom in 1980 to twice that percentage nine years later. But the tremendous rate of growth sustained in the 1980s (partly because of the huge Chinese charismatic growth) is not forecast to be sustained in the 1990s, though Pentecostal growth is still a very major factor, and one which cannot be ignored. One church person in four in 2000 will be Pentecostal/Charismatic.

Table 2 also shows that the rate of growth of the non-Pentecostals/non Charismatics is increasing as the century closes, showing that growth is not purely related to these groups. In Europe, Pentecostals are important and growing in the main (though not in Norway)[3]. In England, Pentecostals are a major source of growth but the Independent churches have also seen expansion - including both the Charismatic and non-Charismatic wings.

Growth can occur anywhere! The principles of church growth should, therefore, continue to be taught, as well as the implications that follow growth in terms of coping with leadership pressures, priorities and structures.

2. The Increasing Number of Churches and Denominations

In what groups is this growth in Christianity worldwide taking place? Which denominations are seeing the greatest changes? David Barrett estimates these as well[4].

There are two groups which are growing - the non-white indigenous Christian and 'others' which include many small denominations. These two categories share similar characteristics - their churches are frequently small, often started by specific church planting, evangelical, autonomous, sometimes autocratic and very active.

They will not necessarily meet in a specific church building. In South Africa, for example, there are nearly 5,000 distinct black Zionist or Zionist-type congregations many of which meet on Sundays in colourful clothes in fields, beside the roads or wherever space can be found.

Turning from the worldwide scene to Britain, we see the same pattern here, and to an increasing extent in Europe. The House Churches form the edge of this rapid growth. Active movements like DAWN (Discipling A Whole Nation), and March for Jesus, spearhead the impetus to plant churches.

At a Conference for Church Planting held in May 1991, the then new Archbishop of Canterbury, George Carey, encouraged 'all parishes of moderate size to consider church planting in their own area' [5].

It may well be that the stimulus of the Decade of Evangelism (or Evangelisation), as the 1990s have been described by most major denominations, will also lead to an increased number of new churches.

House Churches, many of which prefer to be called 'New Churches' [6], began as a break-away movement in Britain in the late 1960s and early 1970s, meeting initially in homes. Today collectively they form a major grouping in the United Kingdom.

They are divided into a number of key fellowships of between perhaps thirty and one hundred or more churches each - Ichthus, Pioneer, New Frontiers, Team Spirit, Cornerstone, Covenant Ministries, Plumbline. These are all evangelical, independent and charismatic.

Many other non-denominational churches follow their example. These churches are frequently single church fellowships or at most a group of two or three fellowships who are 'not covered' by New Church leaders.

The different rates of growth for the 'New Churches' and Afro-Caribbean (as the 'non-Western indigenous Christians'

are called in the UK) and other Pentecostal churches are
reflected in Table 3 [7,8], many of which have to be estimated.

Table 3 : *UK Church Members by Selected Denominations
1980-2000*

| Denomination | Church members | | | Average percentage change per year | |
	1980	1990	2000E	1980/ 1990 %	1990/ 2000 %
New Churches	20,000	120,000	200,000	+19.6	+5.2
Other non-denominational churches	5,000	70,000	100,000	+30.2	+3.6
Afro-Caribbean	65,000	70,000	85,000	+0.7	+2.0
Pentecostal	89,000	96,000	111,000	+0.8	+1.5
All other denominations	7,349,000	6,408,000	6,174,000	-1.4	-1.2
Total Church members	7,528,000	6,764,000	6,174,000	-1.1	-0.9

These figures of rapid growth by the smaller denominations must not be taken to imply that other denominations in
the UK are not growing. Some, like the Baptists, are. So are
smaller groups like the Seventh-Day Adventists who doubled
their numbers in the urban areas in the 1980s.

But the churches in Table 3 are the ones showing the fastest
growth over the last twenty years of the 20th century. The
number of churches or congregations in these groups [9] gives
a better impression of their church planting work, as can be
seen in Table 4.

Whilst the other denominations collectively have fallen by
4,000 congregations between 1980 and 2000 (largely due to
Methodist and Anglican church closures), the New and
Pentecostal Churches have seen an increase in excess of 5,300

congregations. Such small independent churches depend tremendously on the quality of their leadership. The autonomy of so many Christian congregations will worry some.

Table 4 : *UK Congregations by Selected Denominations 1980-2000*

Denomination	Congregations			Average percentage change per year	
	1980	1990	2000E	1980-1990 %	1990-2000 %
New Churches	190	1,400	2,500	+22.1	+6.0
Other non-denominational churches	150	2,000	2,600	+29.6	+2.7
Afro-Caribbean	840	970	1,240	+1.4	+2.5
Pentecostal	1,200	1,290	1,410	+0.7	+0.9
All other denominations	47,610	45,260	43,620	-0.5	-0.4
Total Church members	49,990	50,920	51,370	+0.2	+0.1

This then is the major area of growth today in Britain, in Europe and throughout the world. Major denominations like the American Southern Baptists are encouraging church planting and some, like the Christian and Missionary Alliance in countries like Guatemala, have seen spectacular success. But the most rapid growth is in the independent Pentecostal/ Charismatic sector.

The major inference that emerges from this examination is that today our churchmanship seems to matter more than our denomination. What we stand for increasingly counts for more than what we are called. This is so for those who would not necessarily call themselves evangelical. One minister said he was broad first, Anglican second. Another might state he is liberal, then URC. A high churchman is primarily just that.

This emphasis is likely to continue into the 21st century and it means we will need to know why we believe what we believe. Focusing on churchmanship rather than denominations means looking less at tradition and more at the core of the gospel. This emphasis is much more likely to be seen in the Anglican and Free Churches than the Roman Catholic and Orthodox, but will not be totally absent from these either.

3. The Increasing Impact of Non-Western Christianity
Who might have guessed 30 years ago that in 1990 over a quarter of the world's missionaries in 1990 would be coming from Two-Thirds World (or Third World as some call it) countries and ministering in other Two-Thirds World countries? Larry Pate in his useful book *From Every People* [10] not only documents these numbers but projects a vast increase by the year 2000. Patrick Johnstone in *Operation World* [11], defining a missionary as a non-cultural worker, gives smaller numbers but supports the trend. Of the 68,000 missionaries serving in the world in 1980, 11% came from the Two-Thirds world [12]. By 1990 the percentage was 26% and by the year 2000 perhaps 40% [13] of the estimated 100,000 missionaries will be from the Two-Thirds World. Some of these missionaries serve in the Western World also, and their emphases are, therefore, beginning to make an impact, if only slowly, on British Christianity.

The British and Europeans are no strangers to non-Western ways. Immigrants have been coming to European countries for many years, especially to France and Germany. There are 2,000,000 ethnic Volga Germans in the former Soviet Union, many of whom might wish to go to a united Germany, especially since there is little chance of the German Volga Republic being recreated in Russia [14]. About a quarter of a million immigrants come to Britain every year, about 1 for every 250 of the population. The large majority are Western; between 10% and 20% are not. Some of the non-Westerners, and many who come from Africa or the West Indies, are Christians. These started their own churches in the 1950s and 1960s when ostracised by white congregations. Today many of these Afro-Caribbean congregations have regular white visitors and white members. The New Testament Church of God has several white ministers. Many non-white people also now worship in white churches and find a genuine welcome which was absent 30 years ago. Generally, non-white Christians are Charismatic or Pentecostal, with an exuberant faith which is highly infectious! Practical, forceful preaching is another hallmark, though this has not been copied so avidly.

The Chinese Churches have laid a special emphasis on reaching the Chinese in this country, and in 1990 had 45 congregations. The Korean community is smaller, but there were 17 Korean churches in Britain in early 1992. Their involvement in local mission, church council gatherings and in leadership forums has made the impact of their dedication to outreach very real.

One church in every 41 in Britain in 1990 was a non-Western church. If present trends continue, one church in every 34 will be non-Western by the year 2000. Their influence is definitely increasing. What is the nature of that influence? What example do they set? The English Church Census[15] report suggested their strengths include:

1. High degree of commitment to their churches. When people find themselves living in a different community this is not unusual.

2. Attractive worship, culturally relevant to those who come.

3. Unity, especially through organisations like the Afro-

Caribbean Evangelical Alliance and the Chinese Churches
Overseas Mission.

4. Homogeneity through similarity in age-structure. 60%
of Afro-Caribbean attenders were of working age (20-64) in
1989 and only 6% were over 65 years of age.

5. Similarity in residential areas and lifestyles and thus
easier 'people-group' evangelism.

4. The Increasing Number of Christian Organisations

When Tom Houston, the International Director of the Lausanne
Committee on World Evangelisation, was asked what were
the key trends in Christianity in the last 25 years, his second
was the increasing number of Christian organisations (his first
was the growth of the Pentecostal Movement). This trend is
apparent in every continent, as often lay people get together
to start an organisation dedicated to outreach (perhaps through
a bookshop or a new literature agency or mission) or to service
the Christian community (such as by focused provision of
visual materials, professional societies, or co-operative information ventures), or to render help to the wider social community (through, for example, running homes for the disadvantaged, conference centres, or general benevolent organisations).

The impact of so many groups working alongside the
church can be considerable, and sometimes is a distraction to
the church. Ray Bakke [16] has suggested that the church's
functions are worship, evangelism, nurture, fellowship, mission and service, and that every church will need to be
involved in all of these to a greater or lesser extent. A
parachurch agency might well engage in one or more, but
never in all six activities. We need to remember too that Jesus
said, 'I will build my church' [17] not 'I will build my parachurch'.

Nevertheless, the increasing numbers cf parachurch organisations are making their collective weight on the church

considerable. David Barrett estimated[18] that in 1980, 64% of the money given to Christian work by church members went to churches and 36% to parachurch agencies. By 1991 these proportions were estimated as 52% to churches and 48% to parachurch agencies and if present trends continue by the year 2000 will have become 45% to churches and 55% to parachurch agencies. That represents a significant shift of emphasis which will encroach on church finances and make it increasingly difficult for them to maintain existing property, programmes and people.

The additional money donated to parachurch agencies comes partly because of the increasing number of them. New organisations attract some money, but tend to divert giving to established societies. Consequently some of the older organisations find it very difficult to obtain the finance they need, and close down, or merge together, or form new societies. The newer organisations themselves, however, are not immune to financial pressure and if the British experience is paralleled elsewhere a number of these will fail after five or ten years.

The British experience can be monitored fairly precisely because of the regular publication of the UK Christian Handbook. The following table shows how the number of organisations has increased since 1982:

Table 5: *The Number of UK Parachurch Organisations 1982-1991*

Year	Total number organisations	Percentage founded prior to 1990	Percentage with no full-time staff	Percentage registered with Charity Commission	Estimated total income £
1982	2,402	22%	23%	41%	350,000,000
1984	2,989	22%	23%	47%	475,000,000
1986	3,580	19%	27%	48%	600,000,000
1988	4,074	19%	24%	48%	750,000,000
1991	4,738	17%	22%	55%	1,110,000,000

The total number has almost doubled in nine years, though not all will be new organisations - some will simply not have been included in earlier volumes. Between a fifth and a quarter work with volunteers only; the average number of paid employees in organisations with full-time people was 14 in 1982 and 17 in 1991.

The increasing percentage listed as registered with the Charity Commission partly reflects the editorial policy in excluding very small organisations but also reflects the increasing importance of the regulatory body. The average income per organisation was £146,000 in 1982 and £147,000 in 1991 if five very large organisations are excluded. This lack of real increase in a period when inflation rose 55% underlines the financial harshness so many feel.

In 1991, 20% of the organisations worked in the services area, 29% in the media or literature area, 14% were directly involved in evangelism at home or abroad, 14% provided accommodation, 7% gave training, and the remaining 16% were church-related organisations. If the trend in numbers continues, then by the year 2000 the United Kingdom will have over 7,100 Christian organisations! Truly a plethora of activity - but how much of it will be helping to win the world for Christ?

5. The Increasing Role of Women

There is a greater proportion of women in church today perhaps than ever before. In England in 1989[19], 58% of those attending church were women, against 55% in 1979. If present trends continue in England the proportion of women will increase further to 60% by the year 2000[20]. In Wales the proportion of women in church (in 1982) was already higher than in England at 62% and in Scotland (in 1984) it was 63%.

There is also much comment about the question of women

in ministry, some dividing the issue theologically between the woman as a priest and the woman as a leader, with acceptance of the latter role but objection to the former. 'The bitter arguments aroused by this subject are regarded with some bewilderment by Christians in Britain's mainstream Free Churches, most of whom have allowed the ordination of women for many years.' [21] The Salvation Army, for example, has had an integrated gender structure right from its formation in 1865. The Church of England agreed in 1975 that there were 'no fundamental objections to the ordination of women to the priesthood' [22], but have been debating the issue ever since!

It is interesting to look at the relationship between women attending church [23] and women in the ministry [24]. Table 6 gives the figures:

Table 6: *Women in Church and Ministry by Denomination in England*

Denomination	Percentage of women in church	Percentage of women in ministry 1990
United Reformed Church	63%	16%
Methodists	63%	10%
Anglicans	61%	5%
Baptists	60%	3%
Other Free Churches	59%	51%
Afro-Caribbean Churches	59%	39%
Pentecostals	56%	2%
Orthodox	56%	0%
Roman Catholics	55%	0%
Independents	51%	1%
All denominations	58%	9%

For those denominations whose female attendance is in excess of 58%, the percentage of women in the ministry is on average 13%, but for those with fewer than average women in church, the percentage of women in the ministry is 0.3%. This could be taken to suggest that the more women ministers there are in a denomination the more women there are in the congregations, and also of course that the more women ministers there are in a denomination, the fewer men are in those churches. If this is a genuine correlation (and more research is required to substantiate it) then we have to ask why this might occur. Is it because men don't like being led by a woman or being preached to by a woman?

In the German Evangelical Lutheran Church women have been able to be ministers since 1976. Since that time whilst the number of women coming forward for ordination has increased, the num-ber of men has dropped. Is this but a reflection of the same issue?

The balance is not reflected in British Theological Colleges and Bible Schools where of the 7,200 places available in 131 institutions, 56% are for men and 44% are for women[25]. Many of these women will serve overseas! 56% of the missionaries serving abroad in 1991 were women. There is, therefore, a greater equality in training for service abroad than for service in the home ministry.

That women would work abroad, and were especially welcome to do so was recognised by Bishop Festo Kivengere of Uganda. 'In (May) 1981, Bishop Festo told his diocesan synod of his decision to ordain women. After lengthy discussion, synod backed him by 300-4 votes. This was the support Bishop Festo wanted.

He wrote to the Archbishop (who had already given his go ahead) and the bishops of Uganda telling them he was going ahead to exercise his episcopal prerogative and ordain women, and inviting comments based on the Bible or theology. Only one responded, though there were plenty of private grumblings that the Church of Uganda should wait for the Church of England... When this was reported to Bishop Festo, he exclaimed, 'If we do that, we'll wait forever!'

'On his return (from the United States) he ordained, on 11 December 1983, three of his lady deacons to the priesthood - the first Anglican bishop in Africa ever to do so'[26].

6. The Increasing Scarcity of Resources

Reference has already been made to the depletion of financial resources available to churches and to the difficulty caused to parachurch agencies generally by the constant creation of new organisations. But money is not the only resource that is becoming scarcer in the 1990s and likely to become more so in the 21st century.

The Church of Jesus Christ faces the future with fewer leaders, both at home and abroad. In Britain the number of missionaries going overseas has been declining since the figures were first counted in 1972. That year there were 7,000 missionary members of Protestant societies. By 1980 the number had dropped to 5,400[27]. There was an identical figure in 1991 despite predictions of a fall to 5,200 by 1992[28].

A detailed study on missionary personnel[29] showed that at least 9% of short-term missionaries became long-term missionaries given a gap of a year or two for further training. There were especially high numbers of short-termers in 1986[30] and these are likely to have kept the total number of missionaries static in the early 1990s. But the underlying trend for British Protestant missionaries is undoubtedly down, and may reduce to 4,500 by the year 2000[31].

British Roman Catholic missionaries were not counted in total prior to 1982, when there were 1,800. Their trend is similar to the Protestants, and there are likely to be 1,500 by the year 2000. This British trend is to some extent reflected in other Western countries [32].

The number of ministers is also changing and not just in Britain, as the following table shows. In it 'state church' includes the Anglicans and Presbyterians in Britain, the Lutherans in Finland, Denmark and Norway, and 'other churches' includes all Free Churches, Orthodox and all non-Roman Catholic churches:

Table 7 : *Number of Ministers, Catholic and non-Catholic in Selected Countries in Europe 1980-2000*

	Protestant State Church Ministers			Roman Catholic Ministers			Other Church Ministers		
	1980	1900	2000E	1980	1990	2000E	1980	1990	2000E
Finland[33]	1,259	1,444	1,631	17	15	13	592	705	818
France[33]	-	-	-	42,561	25,950	11,300	2,366	2,895	3,435
Denmark[33]	1,809	1,898	1,992	112	113	114	275	293	313
Norway[33]	1,258	1,274	1,291	50	47	45	1,461	1,387	1,306
French Switzerland[33]	-	-	-	672	543	433	705	751	789
Spain[34]	-	-	-	31,398	28,152	24,832	650	1,696	2,709
Austria[35]	-	-	-	5,641	4,976	4,344	377	496	622
Irish Republic[36]	-	-	-	3,751	3,384	2,985	362	381	395
United Kingdom[33,37]	18,369	17,179	15,672	7,642	7,630	12,226	10,380	14,387	18,336
Total	22,695	21,795	20,586	91,844	70,810	49,292	17,168	22,991	28,723
Percentage change		-4%	-6%		-23%	-30%		+34%	+25%

This table shows the drastic drop in the number of Roman Catholic priests, epitomised perhaps in France where in 1950 there were 1,000 ordinations per year which had fallen to less than 100 by 1990. The state Anglican and Lutheran churches are also losing ministers, and it is only the smaller Other Free Churches where numbers are increasing, but they are doing so rapidly. This again reflects the impact of the Pentecostal and Independent New Churches; the more traditional Presbyterian and Methodist churches see decline over this twenty-year period, with the Baptists a very slight increase. The figures also show that these changes are European and not just British.

This change in numbers might not be so drastic if there was a relieving army around the corner. Some see women in the ministry as that relieving army and it may prove to be so. The more normal place to look would be in the number of young people in the church. Unfortunately it is this group which is leaving the church most rapidly. In 1979, 13% of England's teenagers attended church; by 1989 only 9% did so - and a 4% drop from 13% is a very high proportion.

Do they come back in their twenties? There is no evidence to suggest they do. Those in the twenties were the group most outside the church in 1989 - 94%[38] did not attend, both men and women. It is, of course, precisely these age-groups with which the Asian and Latin American churches abound. Maybe some will come to Britain as missionaries and attract young people back into our congregations.

Whilst the worldwide church expands, therefore, in the West we face difficulties and acute priority challenges. Finance is falling, ministerial numbers in the established denominations are dropping, missionary numbers are lessening, and the potential for recruitment in our church attendance is small. This is a challenge to prayer, to change and to our vision - where are we going? If we don't like the answer, what do we do now to alter it?

7. The Increasing Mobility of Church Attenders

The next trend is more difficult to identify and virtually impossible to quantify with exact numbers. It refers to the increasing number of people who may go to a church of one denomination this week, one of another the next week and to a third the week after.

The reason for such extreme volatility may be questioned but the fact of it cannot be. The Bishop of Southwark said in 1990, 'We have moved from where Christianity is culture to where Christianity is choice.' That statement, I believe, is true. There is, however, an age element locked within it. Those for whom Christianity is culture were largely over 45 in 1990 and those for whom Christianity is choice were largely under that age.

Peter Kaldor has investigated this phenomenon of 'switching' as he calls it in a brilliant study undertaken in Sydney, Australia in the late 1980s[39]. Every attender of every church of seven denominations completed a form one Sunday morning and gave details of his or her past churches. As a consequence he was able to identify key movements between denominations and how many went which way.

Such research urgently needs replication in Britain and other countries. He summarised his results in the following diagram[40]. This diagram does not show the age or gender of those transferring but these could be readily extracted from his data.

NB: The figures quoted below the percentages of transfers within New South Wales that occur along the paths in question.

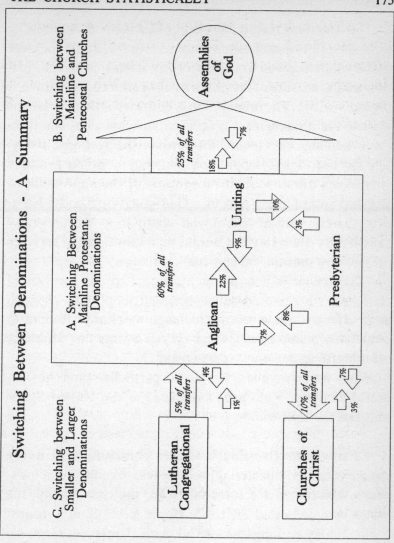

Switching Between Denominations - A Summary

A. Switching Between Mainline Protestant Denominations

B. Switching between Mainline and Pentecostal Churches

C. Switching between Smaller and Larger Denominations

Assemblies of God

25% of all transfers — 18% / 7%

60% of all transfers

Uniting — 9% / 10% / 3%

Anglican — 22% / 7% / 8%

Presbyterian

5% of all transfers — 4% / 1%

Lutheran Congregational

10% of all transfers — 7% / 3%

Churches of Christ

Young people especially choose their church just as others might choose a favourite garage - you go to the one which gives you the best service. Such young people, therefore, go primarily to get from the church rather than to give to the church, although it is unfair in some ways to crystalise their motives so harshly. Many would not put it so strongly.

The American researcher George Barna says, 'Attempting to foresee future attendance patterns requires some measure of the value received from services by attendees, in conjunction with a measure of the importance of church attendance to the individual... The implication to be drawn is that Christians want to feel that their worship is 'significant', but one-third leave their churches feeling let-down on the average Sunday. The fact that these disappointed Christians continue to attend church is a tribute to their recognition of the importance of worship and of being part of a God-glorifying body. However, barely half of those who claim they are generally satisfied by their services would maintain that the services present any meaningful spiritual challenge.

'The upshot is not so much a threat to the survival of churches - where would truly committed people go? - as much as it offers a fundamental challenge to church leaders to establish worship services and church events that are more meaningful to those who participate'.[41]

What attracts young people to particular churches? A useful analysis [42] of 'baby boomers' in the United States suggests the following:

1. Participatory worship; 2. Contemporary music; 3. Every church member ministering; 4. Business-like but not a business - thus rented accommodation for the church, with the pastor in a dedicated office; 5. Home Bible Study groups; 6. No Sunday evening service; 7. Practical, relevant sermons.

In an international study on nominalism, so far unpublished, Professor Eddie Gibbs of Fuller Theological Seminary, found the following reasons why people stopped attending church - note how young most people are when making this decision:

Table 8 : Reasons for Stopping Church Attendance

Factor	Major influence	Minor influence	Average age when a person left for this reason
Church programmes didn't meet personal or family needs	52%	22%	22
Worship service was boring	47%	16%	20
Had serious doubts about the Christian religion	46%	19%	23
Moved out of area and didn't look for a new church	44%	19%	21
Disagreed/couldn't live with the church's moral teaching	34%	19%	24
Few others there of similar age or background	29%	27%	21
Congregation not welcoming	24%	22%	22
Church demanded too much	22%	20%	26
Disagreement with church member(s)	20%	10%	26
Was expected to make too many commitments	19%	24%	26
Disagreement with minister/pastor	13%	5%	23
Ill for a long time	9%	91%	23
Looking after elderly/dying parent/relative	8%	6%	29

In Britain in 1979, 11% of the population attended church, with 8% already church members. The other 3% were [43] still visitors, finding their way, considering their commitment and so on. Ten years later, 10% of the population went to church and 9% were church members. Only 1% were newcomers. In those ten years, the percentage of these new visitors dropped from 3% to 1% - a difference of one million people. Half of them had become church members; the other half had left. The church attendance percentage drop from 11% to 10% was actually 513,000 people - that's how many we have lost. Collectively we have lost our attractiveness.

If Christianity is to increase, it will be by people joining us because they want to, because they see love in action. Bridges must be built into the non-Christian world. When Stopsley Baptist Church in Bedfordshire appointed a second full-time person they took on a community worker who has spent his time talking to and working with disadvantaged families in the neighbourhood. After several years that policy paid off, and the church is now full to overflowing. Here then was a Christian social worker pointing people to Christ.

Our arms are Christ's arms, our legs his legs, our mouth his mouth. We need to become more holistic, more involved with the real world, more dedicated to social issues, more concerned to see justice truly done, more willing to play a part to change society - and in that process may find our church becomes so attractive that people will choose to come, and hopefully will choose to stay.

At the other end of the spectrum, there is a group who do not transfer - those over 65. By and large these people prefer to remain in their own church. One deacon wrote to me, 'I am 78 and the youngest member in our church. All we want to do is die here'. Close such a church, as the Methodists have done frequently over the last decade in the interests of financial viability, and the members stop going, a kind of church attendance suicide.

This trend is likely to continue into the 1990s and the 21st century also as the current English Church population ages. 12% of church members alive in 1990 are likely to be 'promoted to Glory', as the Salvation Army delightfully phrases it, by the year 2000. That 12% offsets the expected 5% rise in church attendance.

We, therefore, have two challenges - to help the young people to choose the church and to help the elderly to change the church.

8. The Increasing Retreat from Traditional, Biblical Christianity

In 1982, Dr Robert Towler, now Religious Affairs Adviser at Channel 4, but then lecturing at Leeds University, conducted a very detailed survey of 1,500 people in terms of their supernatural belief, called the Leeds Common Religion Survey. The results have not yet been published in detail but one question asked about the religion you had, your parents had and your grandparents had. The results are given below [44]:

Table 9 : Religion Across Three Generations

	Anglican	Free Church	Roman Catholic	Non-Christian religions	No religion
Grandparents	60%	14%	20%	5%	1%
Parents	61%	14%	17%	5%	3%
Self	28%	13%	28%	8%	23%

There is little change between the religions of the grandparents and the parents, but there is between the parents and the present generation. The change is largely a decrease in Anglicanism and the increase in 'No religion'. Much of Anglican church membership is nominal, and this result suggests that the nominalism of yesterday begets the agnosticism (or atheism) of today. The implication, of course, is that the nominalism of today will beget the agnosticism of tomorrow. Similar figures would undoubtedly emerge in continental Europe.

'Agnosticism' is perhaps not the best word. Strictly an agnostic is one who feels he cannot know God but accepts that there may be a God. Today the New Age movement is bringing the unknown God to town and promising revelations of his will for our lives through tarot cards, the stars, jewellery radiance, channelling and a myriad other ways. How many are genuine believers in the New Age it is impossible to tell. The Leeds Common Religion Survey found 75% looked at their stars in 1982 but only 19% believed them. Both figures would be higher ten years later. 65% had experienced Palmistry then, 20% believed in tea leaves, 11% astrology and 8% Tarot cards. Almost certainly these figures will have significantly increased in the next decade [45].

Martin Marty, a US church historian, speaking to a Southern Baptist conference in February 1991 said, 'Our biggest problem is not secular humanism but interest in religion that does not turn into commitment' [46]. Can such 'latent worshippers' be brought into a church? Yes they can [47], often because of a move into a new area. 'Dislocation growth' was one of the growth features which emerged in the English Church Census [48].

The escape from traditional Christianity has been aided by the decline in Sunday School attendance. In 1960 perhaps 20% of children attended Sunday School; in 1980 it was perhaps 10% [49], in 1990 7% and by 2000 is likely to be 4%.

The parents of the 1960 children had mostly attended Sunday School in their youth and although their children did not, some memory of Bible passages remained and was transmitted to their children. These children have children of their own now, and such Bible memories as they have have not been passed on, so that, with the general failure of Religious Education classes at school to supply this missing element, many of those aged 25 or under now have virtually no Bible memory. They cannot give the names of the Gospel writers, and ask questions like the young lady to a jeweller, 'I like that one with the cross. Why has it got a man on it?'

What is the Bible memory that has been lost? Studies of those now in their middle age show that most (72%) believe in God and a personal God who is a Father, Judge, Redeemer[50]. Most (89%) will accept that Christ was a good person and many (43%) will accept he was the Son of God. Many will accept the Bible as 'an inspired Book' (as Shakespeare was inspired), will own a Bible and will not throw that holy book away. They accept the importance of religious education (because of the ethics involved). Their theology falls down, however, on the person and work of the Holy Spirit. 'It is a force for good' they will reply when asked about him, never realising he is a person who indwells, sanctifies and enables us to serve Christ.

In a series of Values studies across the world in 1981 and 1982, Gallup showed that people's belief in God increased in middle age (30-60) to reach scores of 60-80% in their 70s. This was common in virtually every Western country. George Barna, a key Californian researcher, suggests, however, that this present generation (that is those under 25 in 1990) will be the first whose belief in God will not increase as they get older because they have nothing to build that belief on. I agree with him. Nominalism is decreasing, albeit slowly. It will literally die out, as elderly nominal church people pass on and are not replaced with younger nominal Christians. When it goes, what was left of traditional Biblical Christianity in those outside the church will have gone too.

At an informal training meeting in December 1991, Professor John Burgoyne, Professor of Management Learning at the University of Lancaster, gave a fascinating, and so far unpublished, overview of trends in the last thousand years. They can be summarised as follows, using his descriptions:

Table 10 : A Historical Summary of Key Characteristics
CHARACTERISTIC

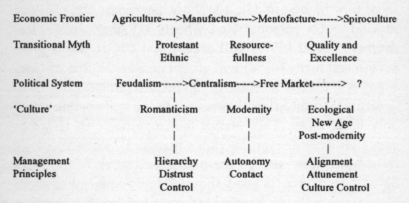

Economic Frontier	Agriculture---->Manufacture---->Mentofacture------>Spiroculture		
Transitional Myth	Protestant Ethnic	Resource-fullness	Quality and Excellence
Political System	Feudalism------>Centralism----->Free Market--------> ?		
'Culture'	Romanticism	Modernity	Ecological New Age Post-modernity
Management Principles	Hierarchy Distrust Control	Autonomy Contact	Alignment Attunement Culture Control

'Mentofacture' means 'of the mind' or 'information technology'. 'Spiroculture' means 'to do with the spirit', possibly 'going back to nature'. If his analysis is correct then we are moving towards a more 'spiritual' era where the culture is reflected by ecological interests, New Age material, post-modernity understanding, bringing with them alignment, attunement and some kind of control over our culture. All this will certainly hasten the demise of the traditional Biblical concepts in Christianity.

9. The Increasing Competition from Other Religions

Between 1979 and 1989, English church attendance decreased by half a million people. In the same period the number attending non-Trinitarian churches like the Jehovah's Witnesses or Church of Jesus Christ of Latter Day Saints (Mormons) or the non-Christian religions increased by over half a million. Not that there was a one-to-one correspondence between the two. But the comparison shows where the competition will be in the 1990s and the early 21st century. The key figures are given in Table 11[51] (ISKCON is an abbreviation for the International Society for Krishna Consciousness):

Table 11 : UK Active Members by Selected Groups 1980-2000

Group	Active members			Average change per year %	
	1980	1990	2000E	1980-1990	1990-2000
Mormons	114,000	149,000	205,000	+2.7	+3.2
Jehovah's Witnesses	84,000	117,000	148,000	+3.4	+2.4
Spiritualists	52,000	55,000	56,000	+0.6	+0.2
Church of Scientology	30,000	75,000	100,000	+9.6	+2.9
Christadelphians	22,000	20,000	19,000	-0.9	-0.5
Other Non-Trinitarian Churches	50,000	43,000	25,000	-1.5	-5.3
Total Non-Trinitarian	352,000	459,000	553,000	+2.7	+1.9
Muslims	600,000	990,000	1,400,000	+5.1	+3.5
Sikhs	270,000	390,000	475,000	+3.7	+2.0
Jews	110,000	108,000	106,000	-0.3	-0.2
Hindus	100,000	140,000	180,000	+3.4	+2.5
ISKCON	30,000	50,000	63,000	+5.2	+2.3
Buddhists	16,000	28,000	38,000	+5.8	+3.1
Other Non-Christian Religions	92,000	152,000	205,000	+5.1	+3.0
Total Non-Christian	1,219,000	1,858,000	2,467,000	+4.3	+2.9

The growth of non-Trinitarian churches is mainly seen in the Mormons, Jehovah's Witnesses and Scientologists. The first two groups are not only active in Britain but in Scandinavia and Switzerland especially. They have also targeted the old Eastern European countries.

The Jehovah's Witnesses were one of the first new religious bodies to be recognised in Poland after liberation. They spread mainly by sending in teachers of English. In Western Europe they have less infrastructure but are still sufficient to be able to be the size of the Baptists. Their growth impetus will certainly be maintained.

Whilst the number of new churches being opened is quite high (300 new Mormon churches between 1980 and 2000) and 800 new Jehovah's Witness Kingdom Halls (usually small) in the same period - one and three a month respectively), their main growth is in trained and active leadership. Commissioned people growth outstrips constructed place growth.

Amongst the non-Christian religions, Islam is marching forward, aided by plentiful oil money. One new mosque per month has been and will be opened in Britain over the last 20 years of the 20th century.

The Sikh growth has been considerable but immigration control is likely to lessen it. Hindu growth is substantial too, with three temples opened every four months in the period 1980-2000 in the UK.

How do these trends compare with worldwide movements? For our final table let us return to David Barrett [52]:

Table 12 : Worldwide Members by Religion 1980-2000

Group	Active members (in millions)			Average change per year %	
	1980	1991	2000E	1980-1991	1991-2000
Christianity	1,390	1,730	2,060	+2.0	+2.0
Muslims	720	960	1,200	+2.6	+2.5
Hindus	580	720	860	+2.0	+2.0
Buddhists	280	330	360	+1.5	+1.0
New Religions	100	120	140	+1.7	+1.7
Tribal Religions	90	100	100	+1.0	+0.0
Non-Trinitarian Christians	40	60	70	+3.8	+1.7
Other Religions	260	240	180	+0.7	-3.1
Atheists	200	240	260	+1.7	+0.9
Other non-religions	710	880	1,020	+2.0	+1.7
Total World Population	4,370	5,380	6,250	+1.9	+1.7

Table 12 shows that Muslims worldwide are rapidly growing and furthermore growing faster than Christianity. It is the Islamic/Christian race that is the major one. We do well to remember Bishop Lesslie Newbigin's words, 'In the twenty-first century, the main global alternative to Christianity will be Islam. Islam will not accept relegation to the private sector as Christianity has - in many societies - so tamely done. Islam, like Marxism, seeks to identify ultimate truth with actual political power' [53].

Sikh growth worldwide is too small to be noticed in this table. Hindu growth keeps pace with Christianity but nothing more.

The various non-Trinitarian churches continue to grow, but their growth in the Western World is greater than in the Two-Thirds World, suggesting there are too many competing ideologies there for them to flourish.

10. The Increasing Political Pressures on the Church

The late 1980s and early 1990s saw sweeping political changes in what was Eastern Europe, the Soviet Union and Yugoslavia. Similar wide-ranging changes occurred in South Africa, parts of central and South America and South East Asia (as Cambodia). They are likely to take place in giant China as the old guard of eight (with an average age of 85 in 1992) dies off. Some changes have been violent (Yugoslavia and Algeria) and others have continued for a long time (Northern Ireland, Peru). It cannot be claimed that the world has changed easily, though the most recent significant changes have been relatively peaceful.

The changes experienced have not necessarily lessened fear or anxiety. The nuclear arsenal of the old Soviet Union, the developing nuclear capacity of Pakistan (outside the Nuke Club), the increasing violence in many parts of the world (America had over 25,000 murders in 1991), do not suggest peace. The appalling poverty in Africa, the colossal debts of the Two-Thirds World, the decline of American influence, suggest time-bombs in the making. The trends of Islam will challenge Christian ideology, and the increasing pluralism and syncretism will merely breed more pluralism and syncretism amidst increasing social unrest.

It was that unrest which Mr. Gorbachev could clearly see as he battled to try and save something of the Soviet Union in the closing months of 1991. He failed but not without warning that it was now possible for a harsher ruler to take over, without the previous restraining mechanisms or political will (or even desire) to stop him (or her). Such a ruler could easily arise and dominate the old Soviet Union, and the old Eastern Europe also.

The New Testament speaks of an anti-Christ emerging before the glorious return of the Lord Jesus Christ. We may not immediately recognise him, as Jesus warned that false Christs would appear before the end came. As with every other age it appears we are living in the last times. Certain scriptures seem to point to our present age as being perhaps closer to those times than previous ages - the gospel has been proclaimed in all the world. Every recognised United Nations territory, all 221 of them, have known Christian churches or believers in them. There have certainly been earthquakes, famines, wars and rumours of wars in abundance during this past half century.

We may not date when Christ will appear, but we are warned to be ready. Tribulation precedes translation. Will Christ find faith on the earth? The hearts of many will grow cold. Children will yield up their parents. But we are called to stand firm, to be loyal to the end, to be ready for death. 'Be on your guard, stand firm in the faith, live like men, be strong! Let everything that you do be done in love'[54].

The Implications of a Changing Vision

We have come a long way. This paper has looked at various increasing factors:

1. Size and influence of the church.
2. Number of churches and denominations.
3. Impact of non-Western Christianity.
4. Number of Christian organisations.
5. Role of Women.
6. Scarcity of resources.
7. Mobility of church attenders.
8. Retreat from traditional, Biblical Christianity.
9. Competition from other religions.
10. Political pressures on the church.

The first five are likely to be more helpful, the last five less so. In differing degrees they all relate to the United Kingdom, to Europe and to the world. What manner of people do we need to be then if we are to keep the faith, complete the race and gain the victor's crown?

We Need to have Clarity in our Purpose

What is our individual calling? Let us pursue it. What are our particular gifts? Let us use them. What is the task the Lord has called us to accomplish? Let us be diligent in doing it.

We need to be crystal clear in our vision. At a conference in December 1991, the British Seventh-Day Adventists agreed to 'establish a SDA presence in 20 new areas at an average of 4 per year 1992-1996, to increase membership by 20%, and to see 3,000 baptisms'[55]. We need to know where we are going, what we expect to happen and to be able to explain that to any who ask us. James Dobson's father was a Christian businessman who interceded much for the work of God. In his will he asked that only two words be put under his name on his tombstone - 'He prayed'. What words do you want put on your tombstone?

We Need to have Tenacity in our Ministry

The backbone of any work we do for the Lord is our love for him and our love for our neighbour. Love never fails; it goes on and on. But the ways of expressing that love may vary. We must be willing to change our ways, our concepts, even ourselves in order to accomplish our purpose - the ministry to which we are called. And change is never easy. Nor are risk-takers always popular. The model we have is nothing less than our Lord himself who was always about his Father's business and could say at the end, both 'I have not lost any that you have given me' and 'It is finished'[56].

We Need to have Courage in our Hearts

We must remember that God's ultimate purpose is to people heaven not earth. We are here but for a short time. We have but one life to live. Let us then run the race, casting aside every weight and every sin. Let us pummel our body so that having preached to others we may not be disqualified. When John Kennedy made Sir Winston Churchill an honorary citizen of the United States, he said he 'mobilised the English language'. At the height of the Battle of Britain in 1940, Churchill addressed the nation. Let us take his words and amend them for our present situation, 'Let us therefore brace ourselves to our duties, and so bear ourselves that if the church and Christ's empire on earth last for a thousand years, angels will still say, 'This was their finest hour'.'

NOTES

1. Rev Dr David B Barrett, *International Bulletin of Missionary Research*, January 1991. Jehovah's Witnesses, Mormons and other 'marginal Protestants' have been excluded.

2. Tom Houston, *World Evangelisation Information Services*, November 1991. Book to be published by MARC, California 1992.

3. See the comparative diagrams for various European countries Figs. 15-22 in *Change in Europe*, MARC Monograph No. 36, MARC Europe, London 1991.

4. *Op. cit.* (item 1).

5. Editor, Rev Bob Hopkins, *Planting New Churches*, Eagle, London 1991.

6. Not to be confused with the Swedenborg churches of the same name.

7. *UK Christian Handbook*, 1989/90 Edition, MARC Europe, London, 1988 for 1980 figures.

8. *UK Christian Handbook*, 1992/93 Edition, MARC Europe, London, 1991 for 1985 and 1990 figures.

9. *Ibid*.

10. Larry Pate, *From Every People*, a Two-Thirds World Mission Directory, MARC, California, 1989

11. Patrick Johnstone, *Operation World*, STL/WEC, London 1986.

12. *Ibid*.

13. Personal estimates for 1990 and 2000.

14. Article in *Time* magazine, 13 January 1992, p.11.

15. Peter Brierley, *'Christian' England*, MARC Europe, London 1991, p.75.

16. Ray Bakke, *The Urban Christian*, MARC Europe, London 1987.

17. Matthew 16:18.

18. *Op. cit.* (item 1).

19. *Op. cit.* (item 15), p.80.

20. Prospects for the Nineties, Trends and Tables from the *English Church Census*, MARC Europe, London 1991, p.24.

21. Ruth March, *Europe Reborn*, OM, 1992, p.136.

22. Quoted from Paul Badham, editor, *Religion, State and Society in Modern Britain*, Texts and studies in *Religion* Vol. 43, Edwin Meller Press, Lewiston/Queenston/Lampeter, 1989.

23. *Op. cit.* (item 20).

24. *Op. cit.* (item 8), relevant denominational tables.

25. *Op. cit.* (item 8), p.662.

26. Anne Coomes, *Festo Kivengere*, Monarch, Eastbourne 1990, pp.409, 347 and 427.

27. *Op. cit.* (item 8), p.439.

28. *Op. cit.* (item 7), p.431.

29. EMA Personnel, MARC Europe Research Report, 1986.

30. *Op. cit.* (item 8), p.442.

31. *Op. cit.* (item 7), p.431.

32. *AD 2000 Global Monitor*, No.11, September 1991.

33. *European Churches Handbook*, Part 1, MARC Europe, London 1991.

34. Mary Lawson, editor, *Spanish Christian Handbook*, MARC Europe, London 1991.

35. Lindsey Mansfield and Mary Lawson, editors, *Austrian Christian Handbook*, MARC Europe, London 1992.

36. Lindsey Mansfield, Boyd Myers, Peter Brierley, editors, *Irish Christian Handbook*, MARC Europe, London 1992.

37. *Op. cit.* (item 8).

38. *Op. cit.* (item 15), p.95.

39. Peter Kaldor, *1986 Joint Church Census*, Sydney.

40. *Lausanne Link No. 4*, MARC Europe, September 1990, p.1.

41. George Barna and W P McKay, *Vital Signs*, Crossway Books, Illinois, 1984, pp.124, 125.

42. *Church Growth Today*, Vol 5, No.5, 1990, p.2.

43. *Op. cit.* (item 15), p.95.

44. Dr Robert Towler, and quoted in *Church Nominalism*, MARC Monograph No.2, May 1985, p.1.

45. Quoted from *The New Age is Coming!*, MARC Monograph No.35, MARC Europe, London 1990.

46. Reported in *World Christian News*, December 1991, p.5.

47. *The Anatomy of a New Congregation,* Church Growth Digest Vol.13, No.1, 1992, p.6.

48. *Op. cit.* (item 15).

49. Estimated from *Children in the Church*, MARC Monograph No.16, MARC Europe, London 1989.

50. Fuller details are given in Peter Brierley, *Vision Building*, Hodder and Stoughton and MARC Europe, London 1989, p.55.

51. *Op. cit.* (item 7, Tables 30 and 31 and item 8, Tables 27 and 28).

52. *Op. cit.* (item 1).

53. Bishop Lesslie Newbigin, *A Missionary's Dream*, Ecumenical Review, Vol.42, No.1, January 1991.

54. I Corinthians 16:13 (J B Phillips).

55. Global Mission, South England Conference, December 1991, Handout *'Goals for 1992-1996'*.

56. John 17:12 and 19:30.